I still look to the sky for answers in a world full of confusion.

I know God is listening, he sends me messages through the moon.

Table of Phases

August's

Supermoon

33 in less than 24
I have been here for almost 33 years
Only been living for 3
It is only the beginning for me
The ending of a chapter
It started to get long-winded
Everything started to look familiar
Until the end
Everything started to change
A good thing
Finally

32 to is ending
On to 33
Well give it some hours
It will happen to me
Damn
I've come so far
This journey has been rocky
Finally, it feels like things are settling down
The life I deserve has caught me
But give that time too
Still have some things to work on
32 has been a Rollercoaster
The end hasn't been so bad
Ended up catching feelings again
Something I felt I never would have
I published a book
A big accomplishment for me
Little Darin is dancing
That was always his dream
More than ever
I'm ready to settle down
And I'm not just talking about relationships
I'm ready to find that balance
I got rid of things I no longer deemed
Me
It was necessary
Stopped talking to people
Peaceful but it sucks at times
We all want that someone
I catch myself checking for a message
This year was challenging
I feel I'm ending it drained
But I'm still happy
Saturday was everything
I needed my people around me
33
I don't make promises
So I'll keep my word to myself
We will receive everything we want
Everything we deserve
And we're not settling

5

Keep God first
Family second
And third my writing
Don't let this life take control
Live it
32 was fun
It's almost done
Let's make it happen in 33

He's different than before
She only remembers the old him
But she wanted to try again
The love is there
She doesn't know if she can trust him again
He understands that
He's working to show her
He's nothing like that
He has nothing to hide
But a text comes in
And she reads the message
All those memories come back
Releasing all the anger inside
Yet he remains calm
He knows he messed up before
But there's no need to yell
Now we're grown
Let's talk about this
She has the password to his phone
Her fingerprint works
She saw the messages before that
Telling that woman he's only going to be with her
She still goes off
He walks off
It takes her awhile
But she goes after him
Thinking he had taken off
He was still there
Waiting
Until she calmed down
Then they talked

I thought about texting you
Seeing if you want to come ride
To skip states
Watching the moon take over the sky
Listening to music
That complements our vibe
To take a break
To put our feet in the sand
To hear you laugh
With the only noise around
Being the waves upon the sand
But I took the ride alone
Recharging my soul
Maybe next time
I'll have your company
As I hit the road

I've been thinking about the past
Daydreaming about your number
Coming across my phone
I still remember it by heart
So when I answered
I already knew who it was
We talked
We linked up
Surprised I moved from home
She could tell I was different
And wanted to experience more
She was everything I needed and more
So we sat up all night playing cards
Talking
Like no time has passed
Like the moments never happened
Creating something
I never experienced before
I snap back to reality
Knowing I'll never hear from her
And I'll never text her phone

At this moment
I realized that I'm the best version
Of me
Nowhere near where I was last year
And who I wanted to be as little me
One or two things missing
But I'm in love with me

I'm in search of balance
To be complete
Finding that stability
That's all I need

Fighting the addictions
Social media
Texting for some attention
This phone in general
I'm not missing anything
People know where to find me

I'm in a different space now
Can't believe I can say this
I made it
I'm happy
But I'm not done yet
Need to stop trying so hard
With some things
Just let it flow again

I am the best version
So far
Can't just give this away
People who deserve this will receive this
It's the only way

I miss the days when we used to sit around and talk
You wrapped up in my arms
Sitting outside until the days were gone
Pulling up late night
Just to ride
Laughing until we see daylight
No I just sit and reminisce
All the days have passed
No one I've connected with
Gave any type of change
And I'm stuck in this cycle
Of thinking of all the things
We did

I miss having someone to talk to
Someone I share a connection with
Someone I can call on the weekends
I can take a ride with
Or even to just come over
And chill on the balcony
Talking life with
I miss sharing moments
Creating new memories
That homie
Lover
And friend
It's challenging now
I don't feel like playing games
So I'll just chill by myself
Counting the stars in the sky
And the little drops of rain

I think my meriods down
I'm feeling moody
You know
The man period
The perfect excuse from the truth
Tonight I'm feeling lonely as shit
I don't want to just call up anybody
Giving away my time
Accepting someone into my space
No that's not it
Not anymore
I wanted to send some text out yesterday
But at what cost
Would have drained me quick
So I find myself in my feelings
Feeling lonely
Yet again
This time I won't just find someone
I told myself not to waste time
So I'll wait
Even though I no longer believe
There's someone out there for me
And that's ok

My dreams will come true
All my goals will be reached
I know what failure feels like
It will not defeat me
I keep getting back up
I am tall
So it was a long way down
No matter how long it takes me
I will figure everything out

I miss my team
The time we spend together
They recharge my battery
Been a minute since we have been together
I mean we spent some time together
But we were all together
Adulting is sabotaging us
Especially me
I have no one else
I cherish those moments
It makes me feel better

Trying not to fall asleep
So much time wasted
But what more is there to do
Nothing to replace with
Plus I am drained
Trying to find the balance
I close my eyes for a second
A Day is gone
And nothing has happened

It's such a beautiful day
Should hop in the car
I just filled up the tank
Roll all the windows down
With the music blasting
And enjoy this day
Go pick up my God kids
Snowballs and the park
Like we usually do
I didn't move that far away
Yeah this heat is draining
But we'll find some shade
I remember one time
One of my God kids ran to me
Sat on my leg
And stole my snowball from me
Then took off once she had enough
That's what I deal with
I enjoy those moments
The time we share
On these beautiful days

Been a while since I star gazed
I just spotted the little dipper
Can't believe I remember that
The darkness of it all
And the brightness of the stars
Forever I can live in that
I placed my feet in the sand
I feel closer
I wish life was this simple
I wish the beach was a little colder
But I came for the peace
I came for the stars
To hear the waves
The breeze that comes along
This time to myself
To feel at peace
To see the stars in the sky
To feel like they're shining down on me

I remember the days when we walked to L&N
From my grandma's house
Two pints of cookies and cream ice cream
And a fifty-cent newspaper
Not for me to read
I just wanted the funnies
One pint was gone during the walk back
One left for the laughs
Dennis the menace
Garfield
Can't think about the other names
But I can picture them in my head
Dilbert
The knights
The second pint was gone
Before I finished
And when I do
I asked for the newspaper from yesterday

Today I read my book for the first time
Since I wrote it
Cringed
I left them the way I wrote them
Flashing back to those days
So I wrote notes
How I was feeling
How I feel about it now
Still upset they left this book in the rain
It's mine now
So I'll continue to read
I still tear up on My Curse
Fear still brings me those same feelings
Cringing
But I have to keep reading

The older I get
The more I think about life
My cousin died
I still have truly cried
Still processing
My momma had cancer
Messed up my mental
I cherish more after those days
I've always been caring
I used to think that was a flaw I had
I shook that away

I have a lot of things I've stepped away from
Even now I'm pulling away
Avoiding the things
That's not happening in my circle
I don't see it
It didn't happen
I drowned myself in it for years

In a period of understanding
And acceptance
Change and accepting it
I'll explain that another day
Just know I don't care
For anything that's not for me
A bunch of God kids
Two are my guardian angels
I love them all
Robinson's and Mack's
I love them all
The family I've created too

Creating a space for myself
Finding more love in it
Allowing myself to be vulnerable
To the ones in it
Sometimes I allow people to enter
When they shouldn't be in it
It happens

So much to talk about
I'm just venting

~venting

I've noticed something tonight
When I see something I like
And I let it walk pass
Something easy comes after
And I would settle for that
Not thing time
I'm not happy with it
I want a wife
I'm not settling for it
I know that's not where it would lead
It's just what I'm looking for
A best friend
A partner
That's what I'm looking for
When it comes easy
I don't see it
Being for me

Everyone wants love
Just not at the cost of losing self
Do people grow out of the games
Or do they stick to their agenda
Nothing wrong with their own ideas of love
But are they wrong for keeping it going
Or the person for sticking around
When things don't match up

I don't believe there's only love
There are multiple versions
Just have to find the one
That matches yours
I could be wrong
But that's how I see love
Not trying to burn out fast
Because I chose to settle
Thinking I can change someone
When they told what love is to them
And what kind of agenda do they have

~the agenda

24

Craving the moments
When the drinks may pour
No not in the club
Maybe in the backyard
With the grill on go
A card game going on inside
Spades or Uno
Bring the kids too
Don't want them to miss out on the memories
But at a certain time
Send them to the room
That's what my parents did to us
Let our laughs continue
Loud
Celebrating life
No worries about someone shooting

~celebration

Cash Rules Everything Around Me
CREAM
Everything around me
I won't move for it
It doesn't run me
But it's a need
Rules Everything Around Me
Love does
Not chasing after the money
It comes to us
We want love
Sharing it with one another
Everything Around Me
Is run by money
Not my feet
I'll take my time
Distracting
Then I'll lose time
But it's a need
Around Me
Is love
Something worth more than money
I'll give it all up for time
With those I love
Those bills won't stop
And neither will time
Love vs Money
Need and want both
But love wins every time

~LoveVMoney

Tonight I was able to count the stars
Surprised with all the light around
Hiding them from my sight
These found their way around
Took a break to pay attention
Wondering what they could really be
Satellites maybe
Cameras because they're watching
Planets in orbit in my solar system
I know that's what stars are
But the far ones
Questions
I still look up
Amazed
Usually can't see the stars
Under the city lights

~looking up

Can't deny that I miss you
You spoiled me with your attention
Fell in love with your conversations
Your personality is one of a kind
Don't think I can replace it
Thought I was losing these feelings
Until you went distant
Showing me the truth
If you were around longer
I would have fallen for you

~Gone missing

You went away
Leaving my life empty
How did I fall so quickly
Just for you to go ghost
Leaving me with a question
With no answers
Thoughts roaming around
Picturing you with someone else
And we're just friends
But I like you
The separation
With no reasoning
You can't come back from
What's the excuse
I won't reply to one
Scrolling to see pictures of you
I allowed you to meet my village
And now you're gone
I can't just let that back in
No matter how much
I want to hear your voice
To hold you in my arms
Soft
Made me soft
Treating you different
I have to be strong
Allowing those days to end
Since you have been gone

~disappearance

She invited him to celebrate
Been years since she had seen him
But she got the courage to invite him
Constantly checking her Facebook messenger
Doesn't seem he looked at her message

He was surprised
Not wanting to open it
In case it was a spam message
Instead he texted her phone
Hoping the number was still the same
She got the message

The day arrived
It was a dinner for her birthday
Smiles all around the table
But she looked worried
The anticipation of seeing him again
And wondering where he was
She sends text with no replies

He showed up 10 minutes early
He watched her go inside
Beautiful he thought
Nervous he felt
Watching the text messages
With no replies

He gets the courage to get out
10 minutes later
Grabbing the flowers
A familiar face
Was getting out at the same time
Greeted with a hug and smiles
He told her he was nervous
She told him everything would be ok
They walked in together

She's watching her phone
Watching the door
Talking to everyone around

And wondering what's going on
Until she looked up again
To see him walking in
She gets up
And all the heads turn

He's smiling
Catching up with his old friend
When his eyes lock with hers
Walking towards him
With a punch to the chest
And some questions

Everyone's watching
Trying to see who that is
Catching on later
Once they both came to sit
He tried to sit far
She wasn't having it

Forgetting about them
He handed her the flowers
Even after the dinner
They stayed together
Catching up for hours

~rekindling

Been a while since I had a heartbreak
This feels like one
More than anything
I feel stupid
I thought I had someone
I let you in
You even have my godchild liking you
Just for you to pull a disappearing act
Good job Houdini
I enjoyed your trick
Bad thing is
You took my heart with it

~fire

It's crazy how quick things can change
It's been a rough week
Today felt the worse
I quit work about 12 times
But I still finished my work
I hope they didn't expect me to stay late
Aggravated
Until I got home
Prayed
Shaved my head
I just knew
Today was going to be a good day
One thing still bothered me
Then I came home
They changed everything
The way my momma laughed
The things my daddy say
And they fed me
Everything's going to be ok
But I think it was a setup
Because I had to get up
And put some work in before I left this place

~home sweet home

I miss the days
When I thought the mailman was 10 feet tall
When the wind blew
It sounded like he was walking along
To let the sunlight peak through my blinds
On Saturday mornings
Just to get up and watch cartoons

~reminiscing

I like to talk though sometimes it's best to listen
And I let her talk
And talk
An empath
I felt what she felt
As soon as these words left her lips
I don't know how much time I have left
It felt as if time froze but life kept going

Perspective
No matter what happens to us
The world will keep spinning
These jobs will replace you
A small memorial in your memory
Only the people that loved you
Will keep your name alive

She keeps living
I make sure to hug her when I see her
Reminding me to give love
To not waste time
To cherish the ones around me

~Life

She finally realized it
The love she has for him
She just hopes it's not too late
She knew it was there
She just hid from those feels
She had to make her way to him
It was early
And she knew he was still sleeping
Luckily his roommate was up
His door wasn't locked
But she knocked
There was no waking him
She smiled watching him sleep
Kicking off her shoes
To hop in bed with him
Sliding in between his arms
Kissing his lips
Waking him to a surprise
He tightened his grip
Pulling her close with a kiss
Both of them drifting off
This is where their love begins

~new love

Earlier I tripped out
Reading a book about death
And I flipped out
Didn't last long
Haven't felt that way in so long
Yet it had me thinking
This is temporary
This is fake
But it is real
I'm living it
To the best
No
I'm domesticated
Fearful
Scared to be me
The fingers are still pointing
Even at this older again
So before death comes
I have to change those things
Live for me and not what they think
Because when that day comes
God will judge how I lived
Not you and me together

~death

Is it still daydreaming if you work overnight
Either way I was lost in thought
Thinking about hitting the lotto
Because working like this ain't it to me
Working for someone else ain't it for me
I can fall in love with Rihanna
Damn ASAP got her
I can DM somebody
Tell them my problems
Fasho they got me
That would be foolish of me
Pretty stupid I think
Nia Long is single
I think
Wishful thinking
Oh how I wish it was that easy
I just hope my dreams will save me
Not trying to get comfortable
Who wants to wait until retirement to live
Domesticated I feel
Working for people who don't really care
The ghetto

~Set Free

Dear God
I thank you for this day
First and foremost
I'm glad I've made it here
I don't know why it's taken me this long
But I made it
Just have to be consistent
Can't go back that way
Remember not to waste time
Can't make that up
And it's only because
You put me through all these things
I've come out strong
Stronger than before
I want to continue to grow
More and more
Cleaning up my mistakes
Making things better for me
It may take a while
I see better for me
May take me until I'm 40
I hope it doesn't take that long
I know it'll happen for me
And it's all because of you
You never gave up on me
I Thank You God
For everything
Good and bad
Thank you

~Changing

There is this woman
She got this smile
That goes on for miles
I have been trying to catch it
Watch it like a sunset
Amazed until it went down
Hoping to see it again

~that smile

This day was one to remember
The night I thought I would forget
I lost my phone too
Thank God I didn't have anything crazy in it
I think
Never thought 24 hours would be so long
We were drinking before noon
Calling it a pregame is an understatement
I mean I forgot the grill was cooking
We laughed about it
We wondered where the smoke was coming from
We had plans to go out
In a different city
So we wanted to see the town
Canceled
The edibles started kicking in
Who wants pancakes
Thank God we didn't ruin them
The Uno game was intense
Someone won
We kept playing for runner-up
Who changed the music
That's when the dancing began
That was all before 6 pm
At 7
Everyone fell asleep
I was the last one standing
Writing with a pen and pad
While she lay across me
Never knew someone so pretty
Could snore so ugly
I laughed
Too loud I had to get up
Plus the snacks were calling me
Just to look out the window
To see my phone
Sitting on the balcony
Where I ended up falling asleep

~story time

As I sit back and watch the sunrise from my balcony
Seeing the clouds turn gray
The orange and blues from the sun rising
The breeze that comes from behind the trees
I thank God for this day
Sometimes it's the simple things I forget about
To be able to breathe
The functioning of my body parts
Being able to see
Though my vision not 20/20
It is a blessing
Even if my day was bad
I am still blessed with these things
I am still blessed with another opportunity to change
Sometimes I forget that
This world is a huge distraction
I forget to appreciate things
Life
The people around me who fill my life
Love
So focused on the negative
So focused on me
I forget
Throughout this whole thing I wanted to say we
But I can only speak for me
I am thankful for these things
Rhonda Phillip Phillip Tatyana
Those 4 make me
Robinson Mack
The family I have created
The same thing
I am thankful for them all

~Good Morning

42

I remember the dream
Not too much of a though
I was in love
With you
At this moment it was official
You pulled up on me
So unexpected
A plate in hand
I wonder what that is
I leaned in the car
Thanks for the food
You smiled and stole a kiss
Shocked
I just looked at you
Can you tell I was blushing
Butterflies were flying
I didn't care about anything
I asked for another one
You let this one sit
Asking if I'm free tonight
You wanted to come sleep
I froze
This has to be a dream
Until a car passed by
It almost hit me
Bringing me back in
I said yes
Definitely
You must have expected that
You parked and walked out a bag
Hugging me tight
Adding a bigger kiss
Holding my hand
As we start walking

~dream love

I've decided to let things flow
Not worried about the outcome
Letting the love run free
Being true to me
Allowing myself to be open
Not holding back from me

I played with myself
For the first time in a while
Turned me on
Was burning up
The feeling after release was amazing
No need for a video
I was feeling it for a while
Put me to sleep
Woke up with a smile

Conversations I've been having
None match one
Two asked for the same thing
But y'all not matching my vibe
Another
Don't worry about it
I know what I like
I'll wait for that smile

I can't wait for the weekend
Either wine or an edible
I have the music ready
Might watch a movie or two
I want to turn my phone off
Something I might do
Enjoying my time alone
Their company won't do

I'm ready for my ride
Next stop
Orange Beach again
I'm staying all-day
Take a nap in my car
On the road again

Just me
The Texas
I want Pappadeaux
Been years since I had it
I'm on the road

I'm not running from my thoughts
I've been dreaming a lot more
I'm not scared
Was in fear
Not anymore
I'm living in love
Just being me
Happy with myself
Just keep swimming

~venting 2

I'm not in the mood
To get to know new people
Sorry
Takes too much energy
Gave my someone my number
Knowing I wasn't going to text
Not like she would want to
Another I didn't even ask
I just like her smile
So I'll just mess with you
The vibe doesn't match what I want
Spoiled
Was on the phone twice last night
I tried right
One said she missed me
But only saw me twice
Telling me she's tired of sleeping alone
I can't give you what you want
I can't even play around
Like that's what I want
Another wants skin-to-skin
Damn
That's all you think about
What happened to the mental gymnastics
That's why I'm so distant
I wish I could go back to that version of me
Jumping in and out of beds
Just trying to fuck something
But I'm tired of giving away pieces of me
I like this new peace in me
Got me out here catching feeling
Pussy
I like it this way
And pussy
Seems like a win-win to me
Anyway

Every day I wake up
And I feel like a part of me changes
Not in a bad way
More toward me being happy

Happier
Comfortable
Like wearing a hoodie and basketball shorts
Can't wait until fall gets to me
I'm challenging myself daily
I'm proud of me
Old me would have relapsed by now
Haven't touched fast food
Thinking about cooking now
Knowledge of what I can't have
Things that leave me bloated
I mean like right now
Take it away

I want to get better for me
Heath wise
Financially
Mentally
And for the second time in my life
Someone else
That's a different story
I wish I could explain this feeling
Like when I knew I was done with tattoos
For a while
Like when I think of things
And I know God is listening
He makes me change it somehow
How sometimes I feel lonely
Not alone
But I know it's so close now
How these writings will save me
Turning more into my everything
And I can stop dreaming about the lottery now
So close and yet so far
No longer going backwards
Though I wish I could talk to someone about this
Then write about it after

~venting 2.5

47

I can touch the stars
I am watching an alien pass by
It was riding on a comet
Playing a weird guitar
I see a Chuck E Cheese sign
On an exit
Is that a sushi bar
First off how can I read this
Yeah
I'm high as fuck

~how high

What if your body wants to be free
The music lets it be
Swaying from side
Flowing with the beat
No questioning of what it is doing
Are you afraid to move it
Posted on the wall

~groovin

The camera pans around the room
Everyone is talking
Everyone is with someone
Then there me
Laughing
Pour up a drink
Someone putting on a song they like
Doorbell rings
Pizza guy
Left a tip
One couple kiss
Another gets pushed for something he said
Funny
Doorbell again
Heads turn
It is for me
They finally get to meet you
The girl takes her away
Could not get my kiss
We keep glancing at each other
From across the room
The sparks between us too
Nobody else is in the room

~like a movie

It's been a minute since I had a thought like this
I blame you because you do something to me
I want you to myself
Soft music playing some candles lit
Some wine that you like
A kiss before and after I want to taste those lips
See which is sweeter
Your lips before or after the wine comes upon it
Lay across from me placing your feet on my lap
Did you throw my hoodie on
What do you have on under that
Let me rub your feet
Can I pour a little wine on that toe I'll lick it off
A little on your leg this time
We can hop into the tube together after
I'll wash you down
I'll keep kissing up until that hoodie comes off
I like what I see no clothes on that skin
Tracing that heavenly body with my fingers
Rubbing your breast squeezing the nipples a little
I'm back to kissing those lips
Already reaching for my shorts
Trust I don't have any draws on under it
But can I get a taste of second base
Before we go all the way
She was like she didn't shave
I laughed and worked my way to the sacred place
Treating it like it should until she grabbed my face
I want you she would say tasting her off my tongue
Oooh I'm in love she's nasty like me
She put it in for me felt like a hot tub
Am I tripping
Slow stroke and she's creaming
Gripping her waist watching her movements
Lean in to suck on those breasts again
Grabbing me for a kiss again
I go deeper in and her facial expression
She's feeling it and I'm lost in it too
Lifting her to grab her ass
While she wraps her arms around me
Stomach to stomach

51

Slow stroking whispering in your ear
How good this pussy feels to me
Hot springs
I need to taste it again and before I get too deep in
She pushed me down
Tasting my dick
Is she an angel or a devil
Deep conversations understanding loving
Now this
Must be a trick
The ring is on the way
I let out an oh shit
She's stealing my soul away
Then climbs on top of it
If I nut quick
We have to go again
I need to get behind that
Gripping that waist with that ass in my face
I might taste that too
With your head on the pillow
Grabbing that hair
Come here
I have some work to do

~sexual

4 in the morning and I'm still up
Went to play with myself because those thoughts
Let me keep them to myself
After I got cleaned up went back into my room
A vision came up
As soon as I laid back down
You rolled back into me
You head upon my chest
Clearly I'm still high
And my bed is still empty
Until I get back in it
Music still playing
I'm not even sleepy
Today
I know what I'll be doing
But in all honesty
I'm ready for that day
I can have someone sleep over here
I want some good energy in my space
Baby rub that booty on me
Take up all my space
Just let me get the wall
Then again you might like my spot
Because it's mine
Fine
To wake up to a pretty face with morning breath
I didn't say it stank
Can't say I'm lonely
Just time to settle down
None of the other vibes are right
Guess I'll wait awhile
Can I get a pack of cigarettes as I wait
Kool 100s or Marlboro lights
I won't smoke them
Setting a scene
Not for me
Guess I'll find a book to read
I don't know where I'm going with this
Guess I just wanted to lay up tonight
Not with anyone
Just you

53

Whoever you may be
The woman who's constantly stalking my dreams
And shutting down any woman
That doesn't fit your description
God planted this vision in me
When I find you though
Those fruits will grow and we will harvest
Because we've been waiting
He made me for you
And you for me
So we will have multiple for generations
Our whole family will eat
Our love will be something special
One of a kind
Two whole and happy people
Keeping each other happy
Being free
Man what am I on
I turned the music off
No need to be in my feelings
Let's talk about sports it's football season
Go catch a Cowboys game with you
Even though you might hate my team
Support me
I'll do the same thing
But if it's the saints count me out
I rather work at a sewer plant
In my boxer and a white tee
I'm trying to spend time though
All my time can't be with the homies
Or alone time writing
I'm trying to give time to you
Wait
Again
Let me stop writing
Because once again
This has become about you
Whoever you are

~all about you

54

Ever thought about your dream day
Like the whole 24 hours you're free
What would you like to be doing
I want mine to be a rainy day
A day when we can lie up on the sofa
Have us a movie day
To see you walking around
In my hoodies and socks
Capturing your beauty with my Polaroid
Why y'all like the peace and the kissy face
As long as you don't drop that popcorn
We're good
Through the time we play
Don't you touch my ass again
Why do women like that
She said you do it to me
Touché
To hold you in my arms for the movie
Teaching you card games
To paint your toes while talking
To spend alone time with you
That's a perfect day

~24 hours

I saw a frog on my window earlier
I was so high I was like
It's the government watch me
Because ain't no way
His eyes looked like it zoomed in
I closed the blinds immediately
Words were speeding through my brain
Visions of different things
A big boom happens
I thought I was tripping
Until I walked out of the room
My brother heard the same thing
I know one thing
My stomach will be killing me
All the stuff I ate
One point I felt too high
I couldn't stand up
The world was moving
The music had me dancing
Straight to sleep
Not too long after
I get up disgusted
Alone another weekend
This edible has me tripping
And now I can't go to sleep
5 am is coming

~rambling

Never knew how much I was done
Until I started to walk alone
Looking at my phone
No one was ready for me to come home
People I can spend time with
Just bad timing
I know what I want

Searching for a song to play
To match this feeling
Wanting to ride until the sun rises
Thinking about those times
Hopefully I can find that again
This time it'll last forever
With her is how my day ends

Every aspect of my life
Is starting to come together
I stopped playing around
Only thing missing
Is my good thing
And this weekend it really hit me

As a kid
I said I would never
In my twenties
I was cheating
Insecurities
Now
I'm ready

I feel like I'm just entertaining
Nothing is coming from this
I'm waiting
Low key tired of it
But I want it
Not forcing anything
Don't want her to settle

Enjoying my journey
Sucks being alone

I can be patient though
Just hope I don't wait too long
Hopefully the connection is deep
Once we meet
Getting to know people is cool
It's really getting old to me

~lonely night

I miss the feeling of love
Hell I miss really like
Give me I want to see you text
In the middle of pool night
With the fellas
I'll holla at y'all later
Give me my date for events
Everyone is like who is this
Deuce
Darin
Loc
She is beautiful
Let's fall asleep on the phone
Only on the weekends though
I need that alarm to go off
Give me a first date
That led to a second
Followed by a third
A few more link-ups
Lead to that L-word
Lust
Turned on from the jump
I really meant love
I miss that feeling

~Lonely night 2

This might be weird
But I miss the smell of the summer rain
Fresh-cut grass on a sunny day
The wind blowing through the tree
The birds singing through the trees
I remember lying down watching the clouds
Sue told me they weren't moving
Learned something different in school
She played me
But where did the birds go
The sun has been cooking us
No rain in sight
Where did those days go
I'll take a trip in a time machine
Just to see those days again

~summertime

She didn't expect the night to turn out this way
It felt like a setup in the beginning
But her heart was warmed at the end

She didn't want to go out
But her girls wanted to get her out of the house
Work and school were her life
Never had time for herself
Tonight that all changed

It was a masquerade ball
They were planning on going there for months
She changed her mind about going
But she had already brought her dress
Her friends insisted they go
Since it's been a while since they hung out
They all showed up at her house at the same time
Music blasting and dancing
She's still trying to get her work done
One stole her laptop and put it up

By the time they got to the party it was after 12
Good thing they brought their tickets in advance
As soon as they walked in they were amazed
The decorations and the lights
Oh and their friend on her phone
In disgust one snatches it out of her hand

First thing they do is hit the bar
Shots
Two for each of them
She's finally starting to loosen up
Her song comes on and she starts dancing

The night goes on
She was approached three times
By three exes

The first one came
Stepping in the middle of her and her friend

Dancing
Wondering how he recognized her
Remembering she left her mask at home
Smooth talking
Trying to buy her drinks
Forgetting that he ghosted her
And cheated on her when she moved in
Once she said no
He called her a bitch and walked away
Fuck him her friends said

The next came
She was walking out of the bathroom
He was standing there waiting
Grabbing her by her waist
A disgusted look came across her face
All he wanted to do was fuck
Asking what she's doing after
Can she leave with him
Saved by the friend

The last one
Was sort of a surprise
They keep in touch
Checking up on each other
But they haven't talked in a while
He spotted her friend first
She took off her mask to wipe off the sweat
They get to talking
He asked how she showed him where she was
Still on the dance floor dancing

He approached
Tickling the inside of her hand
She jumped and looked around
Everyone has a mask on and she can't tell who did it
But something in her
Told her that he was there
Because that was their thing
She turned around someone standing there
A hand reached out to dance

Another disgusted look crossed her face
Until he took his mask off
It was him

She smiled and jumped into his arms
And they danced
He took his mask off and put it on her face
She laughed
He's always been goofy
She didn't mind the sweat
She's been sweating herself

The last song played
They walked out together
Talking and laughing
Her girlfriend's came
They hugged him and went their separate ways
She still smiling
Happy her friends took her away from her place
They hop in the car
Still dancing
Still singing
Next stop IHOP

As soon as they walked in
They noticed
He and his friends sitting there
And as if they could join them

~stepping out

63

This season in my life
Feels like love
Showing love
Giving love
Accepting love
And finding love
This is where my infatuation
With time heightens

I don't want to be too late
Trying to show someone
I feel too late to find it
But I accept all the love given
And I see the fake love
Hiding between it all

~season of love

She wanted a night on town
He was ready for it all
She wanted to do a GRWM
He said
As long as you don't show me in my draws
She did it anyway because he loves to play
Brown suit and her with a dress to match
She said her heels matched his height
He just laughed
The doorbell rung
She wondered who's that
He opens the door
The crew walks in
Dressed to impress
She dances with excitement
Then pushes him
He planned this
Get your stuff together
Let's take this pic
Dinners at 8
After we can go dancing

~night out

65

I thought it was something
How quick things change
I had feelings
I thought it was all for you
It was the things you do
Everything I wanted
Is what you showed me
But personally
It can't be
Nothing like I thought
Still
You gave me the things I want
Hopefully someone can bring that
I can't get what I want from you

~two sided mirror

She was but a muse
All I was able to keep was the painting
I fell for the curves
The facial structure
Made every stroke worth it
She spoke
Making it personal
Bringing the painting to life
Everything she said
Make the colors bright
Well brighter than before
After her time was up
She just left
And I sat there
Waiting for more
Still working on the painting
Though it has been done
I added to it
Things that I wanted
She poked her head in
Every now and then
But she had moved on
The colors started to dim
The feelings changed
But the painting was finished
Ended up back to where it was before
She was just a muse
A muse that I fell for

~crushing on a muse

A fog covers the room
So thick I can see
I try to say something
But my voice has left me
I take a few steps
Still trying to see something
All I see is clouds
I don't want to keep moving
Just in case there's no floor
Sitting in that one spot
Not moving an inch
Scared to move forward

~clouded

This has to be a different world
Than what I grew up in
They finesse me into getting a job
Saying it will be a good thing
And when I'm tired of it
They tell me to just do it
While they silently judge me
When I get tired and quit
I should've moved to Texas
Dallas at that
But I stayed home
When the tigers roam
So I can watch my rugrats grow
While trying to find love
Leaves me colder than Alaska
Windy like Chicago
But I stay cool like Gerald from Hey Arnold

~such a dad

I care for you
Way more than you will ever for me
You could have been the one
Only in my head
You had everything
The total package
But I'm a fool
Falling for false things
Playful actions
Waiting for something
That will never happen
Place my heart on the table
You covered it with a napkin
And just kept talking
Like it never happened
It's not your fault though
I'm the one that fell
Can't expect you to give
When you made it clear
A friend is what I am

~step back

As I lay here
All I can think about
Is you
Foolish of me
To involve my feelings
Knowing they won't just go away
There's another
Possibly a few
That wants to be in that space
I just can't allow is
It doesn't make sense
When all I want is you

~stuck

Ready to let go
But will my feet move
My mind is over it
My heart does what it wants to
This time
They're on the same page
It is time to let go
On to better things

~Letting go

She lays there
Staring
Wondering what's going through her mind
Something about me
The way she keeps looking
Probably wants her lips on mine
Staring
I wonder if she'll say something
Lips open
She doesn't say anything
Just stares
Liking what she sees
Guess I'll lie back down
So she can lay under me

~her eyes

Starting to lose things to write about
Everything is starting to look the same
The clock's hands are moving fast
And the only thing changing is the age
The cycle continues
Schoolwork bills and a little play
That can't be it

So I took off
Usually I go east
West is where everyone is
North it
South has too much water for me
Hit the road at 5 am
No need to pack a bag
I already keep one in the whip
The hoe bag

An hour in
I get to see the sunrise
I stop at a place I've been
I found the inspiration to write something

Cherishing the sun
Its presence takes the morning dew
Off the grass
Changing the reflection of the water
From the black of the night sky
To the red-orange and blues
Of the sunrise

Closed the book
I left my phone in the car
Let the sun grace my skin
Hopped back in the car
I have a long drive
Though I don't know where I'm going

K.R.I.T. playing loud
Windows down
My two eyes saw your third eye

74

From across the room
Every time I hear that song
I think about someone
A muse
A thought runs across my mind
But I refused to write it down

I reach a sign
Now entering Arkansas
I remember this route
I've been here before
The curves
The trees
Is anyone behind me
I need to take a picture of this
I stop in the middle of the road
Tripod set
Single take on
Got it
Time to go

For miles
All I saw was curves
Trees
The leaves changing
Beautiful
Another writing

Can I hug your curves
Like I maneuver through these
Is it simping of me to say
I find beauty in these sites
Though the only beauty I see
Is you

Let me focus on driving
Put hot springs in my GPS
Need to search a hotel
I thought this would be a day thing
But I think I'll spend the weekend
Just me and my backpack

75

Finding all the inspiration I need

~street running

God said he will not
Destroy the world by water again
I feel the heat being produced
Is it too late to fix those sins
Is he about to clean up the mess we made
Or maybe we have been living in hell
We've just been feeding the flames
And wonder why the weather changed
Been a while since I've seen rain
Been a while since I saw good things
Besides on social media
When people are happy every day
Followed by mess
And people's business on display
I guess that's a balance
Must be a better way
Feels like I'm cooking
People passing out
Fires starting
Another variant of COVID
Has to be hell that we're living in
Then there's my thoughts
Wants and desires
Hopefully I obtain those things
Before the flames consumes me
It's a new season for me
A season of love
Showing love
Accepting love
Finding love
Hopefully that brings rain
I know I'll complete two of the three
Just hope I'm not too late
I know this is just preheat

~the heat

Random thoughts run through my head
Some I don't write down
I have to get better with that
I thought about one of my uncles today
Been a while since I saw him
Haven't been on that side of town in a minute
I remember when my auntie and uncle came around
I ran out the back door
I was scared
I remember my daddy used to call me a lot
Can't lie I used to ignore it
My brother had to come to find me
And bring me his phone
Now talk about everything
My how I have grown
One thing I truly miss
Going to North Thibodaux
Kissing my grandma on her cheek
Lying next to her watching her soap
Things may have changed
But it's because we've grown
I may not watch TV with her anymore
I still lay on my cousin's sofa
Watching movies when I go home
Try to see who I can
24 hours aren't long
But I make sure I go home
To hear my momma since
To see my daddy be messy
They say that's where I get it from
I don't think I could move too far
My family is my recharge
I need them

~family

78

My dream car
An 87-grand national
Three years before I was born
My own time machine
Dressed in all-black
All I need is a different deck
I still have all my CDs
Pop in one of my mixes
See where it takes me

~cruise control

She is but a muse
Yet her face and body
Has yet to be revealed
I don't know her name
But I can paint her still
It's a feeling I have
She's close by
Can't you tell
Beautiful on the inside
The words created a picture
Before her face card could fail
I doubt it will
So I keep painting
A colorful canvas
With a black figure in the middle
She is but a muse
Just this time it's different

~new canvas

I fell for this one
Fell flat on my face
Thought she was the one
She was just the prototype
I'm headed the right way
When she walked
Flowers grew in her steps
Her mind watered them
The words she spoke
Just like her looks
Breathtaking
Would have been a fool
If I didn't try
Forgetting there are two sides
Well she had a few sides
Got caught up in the scent
Eyes closed
Taking it all in
Not noticing the water rising
She looked back a few times
And kept walking
If I didn't like breathing
I was a goner
And before I knew it
She was gone
Was sad for a while
The blueprint was made

~prototype

I've been dreaming a lot lately
My mind going crazy again
Wildest one I had
My Cowboys won 109 to 6
Ok
It's time to wake up again
But it has me creating again
Stories I wish I could share
It's not I don't want to
But who wants to read all that shit
Lol
Ttyl
Going back to sleep
Again

~again

It's been a minute since the fellas and I hung out
They're married and we're all busy
So it's hard for us to link up
I need another night's sleep in the Waffle House
Drinks and laughs until the clubs shut down
And we're not even in there
Last night was that and more
Still don't know how I made it to work

No names will be said
just know it there were six of us
Three left early
The wives were calling
The other two had their women with them
That's what I love about my crew
We're all cool
Hopefully I find that too

It was a game night at the crib
I don't remember who brought the Uno flip
But I own them a new deck
I threw them shits away
I hate that game
Everything else was cool to play

We separated into teams
Those that weren't playing
Were playing from the sideline
Should have just hopped on a team
As the night died down
The fellas decided
Let's go grab some drinks
And the night began

We ended up at our favorite spot
The pool hall
Friday night
So it was kind of packed
But we went straight to the bar
First two rounds of shots on me
Brown please

All the pool tables were full
but the darts were free
Each round
The last two with the highest score
Take a shot
The losers of the game take two
I won of course
That's what I'm going to tell you

Phones start ringing
Wives calling
Be safe
Let me know when you make it
Talking shit begins
With their whipped ass

Finally a table open
But I couldn't focus
They laughed as I scratched
They couldn't do better
Talking shit to their women about them
Just trash
My stomach started to growl
Where are we going to eat

Grabbing my phone
Trying to find something open
Three missed calls
A few messages I didn't open
One read wya
Now it's time to go
They just don't know it yet

We walk outside
Planning to go eat
Until a car swings through the parking lot
They wondered who that could be
Sobering up quickly
Not knowing it was for me

When she rolled down the window
And said my name
They all stopped and looked at me
I'll introduce y'all later
They weren't having that
The car they approached

Twenty minutes passed
Still talking and laughing
Blaming me for their not meeting
She wasn't a secret
Yeah ok
Can we go eat
I'm starving

Ended up at the Waffle House
Let me get my Allstar
I don't need to look at the menu
She just stared at me
Is there something on my face
She said she was just wondering
Will I fall asleep here
Like I did on my birthday

They all laugh
I looked at her and smiled
Stop playing with me
Today was a good day

~Night out pt.2

85

Popcorn popping
A bag full of snacks
Don't eat junk food often
Tonight I can indulge in that
A voice from the other room
Yells what do you feel like watching
The Brothers
Been a minute since I've watched that
She agreed
A movie she's never seen
Almost dismissed her because of that
But I digress
Grabbing a few bottles of water
She wants the wine
Then she asks for something else
Your feet work
She said yeah but they hurt
I guess that's my sign
I have to rub them again
All I know is
They bet not be dirty
She laughs
Through some popcorn at me
Once I sat down
If I see a roach I blame you
I push play
Lay in between her leg
Beat her to her spot
And I don't plan on moving
She feeds me some popcorn
Time to watch my favorite movie

~movie night

Early morning
Woke up to the sunshine through the blinds
Afraid the heat would ruin the day
But the breeze cooling the earth
Called in today
My supervisor wasn't there anyway
Either way
I was taking my day
Washed the whip yesterday
So we could hit the interstate today
Made the call
They said it's on
It's on then
Hit the gas station to fill up
Last time I checked
Gas was 3.40 something
Pull up to the pump
2.99
Blessings
Get back into the car
Phone ringing
Call from the woman I've been dating
Saying she's free this weekend
Pack a back
We're skating
Pull up to her crib
She was walking out the door
Got out to open her door
Greeted with a kiss
Placing her bag in the trunk
Whatever she got on
Hypnotizing
Leaving a little later than I wanted
But the way today has been set up
It'll be worth it in the end

~i10

Some days I want company
Same time I rather be alone
Take me an edible
Turn on the record player
Turn the room light off
Let the light from the lamp take over
With the music bouncing off the walls
I work on my Playlist daily
Giving me something good to write to
Don't need anyone to kill my mood
So I vibe alone

~vibe session

Let's say
I call you the most beautiful girl
Would you tell the judge I lied
Make me pay a fine
Or will you believe me when I say it
Smile from ear to ear
Even blush a little bit
Can place my hand on your face
And use my thumb to feel
The softness of your lips
Before I steal a kiss
Can I talk about your complexion
Because you're glowing
Would you tell the judge about me
Saying I'm lying
Sending false information
I'll prove my innocence
Showing how beautiful
You look to me

~you

Can we stay in bed a little bit longer
Watching the sunlight
Kiss you through the blinds
Makes you look heavenly
Not knowing the devilish things
You did in between these sheets
The night before
Can part of our day
Be spent wrestling in bed
I'll make some breakfast
You repay me with a kiss
Can we talk
Listening to some music
While the candle is lit
Spreading a beautiful fragrance
Can we stay here a little longer
Before the day
Takes you away from me

~good morning

She brought what I needed
Which leads to something more
No I'm not talking about sex
Can't say I wasn't hard
But her mind is what I penetrated
The conversations lasted hours
The laughs tagged along
Headphones in
Walking around
Doing random shit
In my early 20s
Maybe even before then
Like I'm on the house phone
Felt like a kid again
I wanted more
But sleep calls
We have work in the morning
The recharge I needed
Hopefully we can do this again
This time in person
At a dinner table
Maybe on a walk after a movie
Or at the airport
Waiting on a flight
Even at night
While we take a late ride

~you and I

I don't want to acquire more stuff
That's a temporary fix
That high doesn't last long
I give it a month
I'll forget about it
I don't want to meet new people
Take too much energy
Just for the love to be fake
I don't have time for that
I just need time with you
Creating new memories
That'll last forever
While we work on forever
Something we'll share forever
Creating a Family
Incorporating our families
That's important to me

~what matters

It's crazy how things change
How I grew from a boy to a man
How I got over those games
And can't move the same way
How I found myself on this journey
How life no longer has me worried
Like how I know I'll make it through
How it's not just about me
I have a we
No spouse
I'm talking about my family
A spouse one day
Had to change for better days
Cheated on so and so
All that's out of me
I don't accept the wrong energy
Can't no time with me
I think sometimes
Going back that way
Shid
Not me
Some things remain the same
The nonprofit I created
Wasn't ready for those days
Can't lead
Doing those same things
Had to do better
I still think about WCA
Writing is still my thing
Obviously
Those days will never change
I stopped once
Can't do that again
Feelings are changing
I guess it comes with this growth

~feeling the change

It made my day
The small piece of you
That the world gave
And like a drug addict
Can I get another piece
Felt so good
I thought it was a dream
Is this what it feels like to be high
I'm floating
I didn't want it to end
Until the sun came up
And I woke up
Damn
It was a dream

~another piece

I decided to sit in the rain
Letting the drops cool my skin
Closing my eyes
Taking the smell of the rain in
Staying in the moment
Forgetting everything that is going on
Around me
In my life
Everything
Finding peace
In every piece of rain
That falls upon me

~sitting still

It's been a long time coming
She's been hustling
I would get a call every now and then
Talking about the dream
I saw it coming
Day in and day out
She was studying
Working two jobs
Saving up her money
I remember the tears
Things were starting to get hard
She wanted to quit
As a friend I couldn't let that happen
Have to keep going
She did
Nonstop
Piece by piece
Things started to fall into place
Next thing I know
I look on social media
I see her face all over the place
She's doing it
She did it
She obtained her dream
The hard nights
Multiple jobs
The tears
Everything
Lead up to this moment
When the dream comes into fruition
I saw it happen
Felt like I was a part of it
But I saw it
Even when she didn't anymore
She was ready to throw it all away
The jobs she obtained
Would allow her to live a certain way
But that wasn't what she really wanted
I couldn't allow her to settle
She'll be unhappy
She made it

She's happy
Can't wait to see where this leads
All I know is
Drinks ain't on me
This time

~her dream

Did this really happen
I never expected this to happen this way
I fell in love
Never believed in love at first sight
But it happened to me

I was walking through the store
headphones in
Not paying attention to my surroundings
Looking for what I'm looking for
A crash is what found me

Searching for a song with my head down
You were replying to a text
When I turned the corner
Everything flew everywhere
I thought an attitude was coming
I did say sorry
Until we locked eyes
It felt holy

We introduced ourselves
talked about what we had
I'm trying to eat better
You're going home to cook something
Something I never had
We walked around talking
I had everything I had
An exchange of numbers was had

Hours passed
I'm out with my friends
They see I'm distracted
Wondering what happened
This woman is on my mind
Never expected this to happen
We just meet
My mind she never left
They see it in my face
They seem happy

Then my phone started to ring
It's a number that wasn't saved
I answered to a voice I didn't recognize
Until she said her name

I was out with a group of friends
You were too
We are at a restaurant downtown
You're downtown too
We should meet up
We just sat down
Y'all should pull up

She walks in
I'm facing the door
So I was looking
It was just two of them
It was a few of us

They joined in
She sat right beside me
Everyone's talking
Shots landing on the table
To us
It's just you and me

We all leave
We took a group picture
Then disappeared
They started to look for us
Until they looked on the level
Their we sat
Laughing
Here they come
Being messy

~a dream

Watching the weather change from my bed
The wind blowing the trees
Thunder roars through the sky
I should open up my window
Just to see if I can get a smell of the rain coming
The sweet smell of the rain
Would probably enhance these thoughts of mine
So I'll keep it closed
Thoughts of my goals in life
Love of course
And the freedom I long for
That starts with me
To continue to break the chains off
It's okay to feel the way I do
Don't have to be afraid
Don't overthink
If it feels right to you
Go with it
This is your life anyway
To let the mind control end
You know all the things they taught us as children
I'm grown now
I can make the rules for how I'm living
No judgement
If I want to lay naked in bed with a candlelit
Looking out the window
Waiting for the rain to begin
To take a pick of myself like that reading
Because I liked how I was looking
I'll do it
Why
Because this life is mine
Can't allow the mind control
Of what I should and shouldn't be doing
Ruin it
Guess I'll open my window anyway
Allow the smell of the rain to take over my room
Probably put me to sleep
A minute before my alarm goes off
I hope I get caught by the rain

I am FREE
Free to be who I'm meant to be
I did some changing
Some searching for me
Came across some things
Shit just didn't feel right
Got rid of that
Shit is starting to feel right
I killed the judges
Only one true judge here right
So why should I fear life
Why should I worry
About what someone else opinion
Of how I'm living sounds like
I sleep in my skin at night
This life is my playground
Well
It's an adult arcade now
Have fun
Live
I know we have adult things to do
But we're still kids
Enjoy life
Be FREE
Be yourself
Don't worry about what they have to say
This ain't freaky Friday
They can't take your place
These my shoes
I wear them because I like them
I wear hoodies in the summertime
For the same reason
I wear draws and sometimes I don't
Let that thang swang
Don't want to see it
Don't look
Hahaha funny
But seriously

101

I'll be damn
If I allow someone
To take my freedom away from me
I am FREE

~to be free

There's beauty in the storm clouds
Can you see the sunset behind the gray clouds
Turning them gray with an orange tent
The moon is shining bright too
Can I take you there
No rocket needed
I'm one with the universe
It'll send a star for me and you
Or we can wait a couple of days
The moon will be blue
With Saturn's rings
I have an umbrella if it rains
Even though I don't mind getting wet with you
Though I miss the stars
I can find the beauty in this

~eyes of the beholder

I'm just getting home
She's up rushing
Said that she was going to be late
I can't get a kiss it's been a rough night
She knows she knows
But she has to go
He watched her car pull out
Then leave
Sad
At the table he sits
Then the door unlocks
She walks back in with a smile
Leaning in with a kiss
I have time to talk
How was your night

~overnight

How high I am right now
I know the nut would be amazing
I feel like I can feel everything
Just imagine inside her would feel like
Amazing right
To feel everything inch of it
With every stroke
We kiss each other
The fire within it
The water that tries to kill it
Then to kiss every inch
Feeling the softness of it
To taste her magic place
Would be crazy

~roaming

You know something crazy
The world could split
In half right now
And the worst part would be
You never got the chance
To be with me
So come dance with me
Don't be so cold
You know what happened
The last time the earth froze
The attitude
That heat
You're the reason
We can cook an egg
On the sidewalk
Sweetheart let me be your balance
Take my hand
No need to be scared
I got you
There that smile go
Now can I take a photo of it
Using my mental camera
Snap
Got it
I'll never lose this picture
Hope we can make a photo book

~talking to you not you

Am I really from the country
Would you call Thibodaux country
Growing up
I remember picking the berries out of the ditch
Washing them off
Sprinkling some sugar on top of it
Going sit in the yard to eat it
I remember breaking the sugarcane in half
Just to chew on it
I remember watching the guys ride by on horses
Going milk cows on field trips
And we didn't go that far
I remember eating watermelon on the porch
A sweet potato pie lady
A frozen cup lady
And a candy lady
Racing barefoot
I remember being able to see all the stars at night
I remember hearing the roaster
When I work up in the morning
I hate that thing
I wouldn't say it's country
I would love to live that way
I do miss climbing the plum tree
And getting yelled at
For squeezing the milk out the figs
My great grandma's tree
I want to live out in the country
Acres just for me
Almost off the grid
Grow what I have to eat
But do I think Thibodaux is country
Am I country
Maybe

~back home

107

Why is the moon so bright tonight
I can't stop staring
Am I about to transform
It's a full moon
With a clear sky
Is there a werewolf inside
No
I just like to look up into the sky
Enjoying the beauty of life

I'm coming to the point
Where I think my wife will be white
Now I know there's no color to love
I just don't think she'll understand
The struggles of a black man
In America
They're already trying to rewrite history
Slavery wasn't slavery
They were some type of workers they say
I didn't listen to the whole thing
And they're trying to take away the books
They think that's ok
She might feel it's wrong
She just won't feel the way I feel things
I'll keep hope alive for a sister

And another thing
Has anyone else been paying attention to the days
How quick they pass
They're blending in so easily
Like my barber if I decided to let my hair grow back
He'll make it like you don't see anything
But I've been paying attention
Today I stepped outside
And the way the sun felt
I wanted to ride around with the windows down
Blasting my vibe Playlist
Starting with the instrumentals

Pay close attention
Fall is coming

108

Cuffing season is approaching
We're trying to lay up this season
Just have to lay down some ground rules
Don't give up any hoodies
A few already got away
They've been replaced
We're not doing that again
It's so hard to say goodbye
But we're stepping out there again
So quick to friendzone

I laid out the plan
Stick to it
Things will be hard
But you'll get through it
Look how strong you've got
I'm proud

~still venting

I'm starstruck by the moon
Can I get an autograph
A picture won't do
What my phone shows isn't true
If I get one with you
I need the clouds and the stars
Around you
See you listen when I speak
You set me a sign before
A falling star
Some shooting stars
I wish upon them too
You send my messages through
The universe gets it
See you dance with me in the rain
Riding with me on those beautiful days
Guiding me through the night

~the moon

You live rent-free in my head
No baggage
So it's a comfortable place
Only happy moments
So when I think of you
Have you ever seen a black man
Turn red
See I like to star-gaze
Spotting the constellations
But instead of the big dipper
I see your face
No I'm not trying to shake this thing
It's meant to be this way
Shows I only want you
And nobody in this galaxy
Can take your place

~rent free

33 and I'm just getting here
Perfect timing
I have the appreciation
Won't take it for granted
Free of that fear
Enjoying this life I live
Have to do more of that
Just being real
We'll get there
Expectation at zero
Hurting myself
So I'll go with the flow
Picked myself off the floor
Thank you to those
Who helped me up when I was weak
I'm strong now
Every man
In the strong man competitions
Couldn't fuck with me now
At all
Where's the passenger princess
We have streets to run
Kick your feet up
Hold on
My daddy calling
I forgot to tell him I was leaving
I love the relationship we've gained
The perfect example
Of the change I've obtained
Has taken some years
But I wouldn't change a thing

~perfect timing

I'm in a space
Where it's no sense of getting mad
Or sad
About things I can't control
Fix it or forget about it
Only time I'm on
Worrying for what
Cutting down on my lifespan
I'll be damn
If stress takes me out too soon
Give me a smile
Laugh out loud
Life is a good
When we're not stressed out
The opportunity
I'm not scared of
I'm not running from nothing
Fruits and vitamins
No fast food
Have me feeling different
Reading
Planning
I'm lifting
My writings I'm posting
Books I'm creating
I'm happy
I'm going to keep going
No sense of slowing down
I took the rear view down
This space I'm in
I've never been
I'm figuring it out
Finally

~creating new spaces

September's

Waxing Cresent Moon

You know
You are not supposed to wear
Outside clothes in bed
It is only right you take them off
And when you lay down
Allow me to visit you
Between the holidays
There's that smile
Been waiting for that all-day

Can I introduce you to my life
I am in no rush to call you my wife
But you can have all my time
I will write you letters
Just so you can save them
For when we get older
Reminisce on those times
Do you remember the time

~starting something

I have been looking for a new muse
Someone to write about
I mean write to
No
Talk to
The conversations do not meet
The quality I seek
So I write them down
Sending them out
Low key slowing down on that
Can't give everyone a piece

~looking

Just looking for someone
To kick it with
Laugh with
I have dreams
Someone to build with
I believe in God
Can we build a better relationship together
Can we pray together
I'm still a kid
Can we play together
I'm a simple man
I enjoy simple things
You'll be the only thing
In my life
That'll be fancy

~still searching

I look out the window
The moon is looking back at me
First time I seen it outside my window
As full as can be
She go sit on the balcony
Having a conversation with it
But my bed is comfortable
An the balcony will hide it
Behind the trees
So I'll open up the blinds
More so I can see
Just me
Talking to the moon

~me and the moon

She called in the middle of the night
I was up
So I answered on the first ring
She was surprised
Didn't think I would answer
But she was glad I did
She was out and she wanted to see me
I'm up working
I don't mind a little company
Surprise surprise
You were already on your way
Hoping you didn't have to call too many times
To wake me
The door is open
I'll be on the sofa waiting
Before I could finish my next sentence
The call ended
The door opened
And there she was
Smiling

~seeing you

Sometimes I think I am over it
Then random thoughts come
Taking over other ones
Letting me know
It is a lasting impression

~stuck

Looking for something new
Calm on the outside
On the inside I'm yelling
What am I supposed to be doing
This can't be it
Waiting and waiting
Trying to figure it out
Searching for purpose
Thought I figured it out
On the outside I'm fine
Inside I'm tripping
Death would be better
This life is hectic
But it's worth living
Still
I need to know
What am I supposed to be doing
Did I go down the wrong road

~wondering

No sleep
Daydreams
Star filled night sky
Trying to beat the sunup
Headed to church
Thanking God for today
And what is to come

~Sleepless

Am I the only one
That still looks up
Wish I could count all the stars
Before I have to break the trance
And deal with what is on this planet

~lost

The world spins
As I dance around the sun
Watching the sunrise
The moon take over
And that's called a day
12 am to 12 am
24 hours of dancing
The songs changing
People are leaving the floor
Replaced with others
The moves changed
Some dance with another
With little ones
Dancing around them
Still I dance
Watching things change
I'm changing with it
A few women to dance with
But I let them slip through my grip
Watching them dance
With someone else
Still I dance
Continuing to change
Hearing the music change again
This is my favorite song
Just waiting
For my dance partner to appear

~dancing

125

First Sunday at church
The men are singing
The guy in front of me
He's clapping at flies
My momma just passed me
Two peppermint
And the only thing I can think of
Is why they have those big red ties on
Keep singing though

Is it fear
Why I didn't approach
Do I feel like I have nothing to offer
Because I do
She was beautiful
Something from a dream
Walked right in front of me
And nothing
But I saw her before
With a man I think
I put this on everything though
I won't let it happen again
Without speaking
If I see her again

~with the braids

I have these ideas in my head
Should I say it
Will it manifest
Or will I taint it
By sharing with the class
The fear is a thing of the past
I still ask
With nothing to say

Every day I look in the mirror
And I love what I see
From the tattoos
To the bald head
I'm the best version of me
Can't compare me now
To yesterday
Change not always a bad thing
Just have to make sure
You like what you see
Wait
Love what you see

~me

I saw a shooting star this morning
The wish never changed
I watched it burst into flames
And burn out before it could land
I closed my eyes
And the wish remained the same
The good in looking to the sky
There's beauty in it
God's still sending me messages
As I talk to the moon

~shooting star

Tired of trying
Trying to figure it out
Trying to find the one
Trying to find something new
Trying to keep things going
Trying to hold on
Ready to let go

~tired

I dreamed that it finally happened
I am finally being seen
My words are being recognized
Just to hear my alarm
Time to get up for work
Nothing has changed
I am still trying to figure it out

Defrosted way too late
This is the cold Era
Wish I would have known better
Love is nowhere to be found
The weather changed drastically
Guess it went into hiding
I woke up too late
Naked
Freezing
Just looking for a warm place

~ice age

The moon seems closer
Feel like I could reach out
And touch it
They I get distracted
Phone calls about bullshit
I am ready to quit
Though I just cannot do it
So I just look up when I can

In a perfect world I'll tell you what my dream would be
I'm 33, finally found me, and achieving some of my dreams
This is a great place to begin
To start I would find my person
One kid would be ok and she'll have some for me
I always wanted to start my own family
She'll be my best friend, my pnc, my business partner, my everything
She'll add to my happiness because I came in whole, I know what I want, and I only want her
Then we will create, not just my dreams but hers
I would stop working, well stop working for someone else
Publishing book, making shirts, my nonprofit going
Whatever she wants to do, if it makes sense, I'm all for it
I would to stop my parents from working
Though I know they don't want that
Get my own land allowing them to do what they want
My sister and brother I can proved for their dreams
I have two cousins I'll help them become chefs
Cooking is what they love, life just takes us in different ways
I would help my nanny fix my grandma house
My God kids, my best friends, close cousins, we'll enjoy life together
Being able to change the weather
No sense of struggling if you don't need to
Only helping out when I need to
I would have two houses
One in Thibodaux and one in the mountains
I would travel the world and learn new things
I would learn how to cook, surprising my forever with different things
I would throw get togethers once a month just to bring everyone together
Life is temporary I would spend time with those I love
I would smile so much more because the stresses I dealt with would be gone
I would help fix my church, take care of my families graves, and thank God every day
In a perfect world this would be my part in it
Just a part of it, I would do so much more

135

The phone stopped ringing
When it does
Hoping it's something I want
Lying to myself
It was never found
Wanting to delete social media
But that's the only way to keep up
Plus to promote my work
Even though
No one reads now
I threw my phone
The ads are taking over
Have to pay a fee to get rid of it
Speaking of getting rid of
Brought a system for 5
Just wondering why
Wanting to take a ride
But I work overnight
I can't wait until Friday
Still wanting someone to share with
Not just slide in for a temporary good time
Wasting my energy on a cheap fix
Wanting to go back to sleep
Hoping this is not it for me
Life has to have more than
Tiktoks
Sex
And cheap pay wages
Think I brought enough hoodies
To stay warm
In this cold world

~still venting

I think about checking in
The only time I receive a message
Is when I text first
Life happens
So I cannot get mad
When I do not cross their mind
My mind always wanders
So I am thinking all the time

Life is being lived through opinions
Instead of life experiences
Social media is where the new teachers live
I wonder what field their degrees are in
There I go
Showing my age
The back in my day
But I'm speaking through my experiences
My own time following the leader
It just didn't live on social media

Dear God
I'm tired of this
I wanted to throw my phone tonight
It wouldn't stop ringing
This can't be it for me
Or is it
I feel like there's so much more
Starting to feel like I'm lying to myself
Chase my dreams for what
Not going to take me anywhere
But I still do it
For a temporary high
Like I'm doing it
To end up feeling nothing
Like why am I doing this
At times I feel like death would be easier
No
I'm not talking about killing myself
I'm just saying
I wouldn't have to deal with this
Sometimes I wonder if I'm really happy
Like truly
I'm nowhere near where I would like to be
Though I have a great village
It's just me
And I feel as if life is moving on
Without me
So am I really happy
Though all those things
The answer is yes
How far I've come
This is the happiest I've ever been
And I don't need
Material things
To complete me
But still
This feeling doesn't change
Tonight I felt anger
I'm exhausted
I find more peace in my dreams
I feel as if this move was pointless

Nothing has really changed
Except my mentality
And I'm closer to my village
I did publish my books
Tired of celebrating these victories
Alone
Everyone I run across seems wrong
Something always wrong
Or I'm not the right one
I'm over it
My time for love is over
I'm done waiting on it
But I don't want to just deal with people
I'm over that
I'll just be alone
My biggest fear has been realized
Being cold has left me in the cold
This would has frozen over
Just hope my second fear doesn't come true
Losing my mind
Living on the streets
God I'm tired
I look around at everything
I feel like the details of life
Is so vivid to me
Like I see everything
I feel everything
My brother is having a child
I have to move around
Have to allow him to be with his family
This job is not helping
My sister is growing up
And is a beautiful young lady
She is looking for love
Messaging me questions about me
Yeah I definitely can tell her what's up
My parents are getting older
I can see it in their faces
I'm thankful I still have them around
And finally
A grandchild is coming around

And me
I liked three people in three years
To where I'll give that life up
To where I wanted to find better ways
To provide for her
Just to end up like this again
I give up
I don't know what's going on in my life
I don't feel like I'll make it far
I feel like this is it for me
God
Sometimes I feel as if you've forgotten about me
I'll keep going though
You know I'll never stop
Though some stuff is beyond me
I am tired God
I don't know what to do
I keep looking to the sky
Hopefully I see a message from you
But I see the stars
And the moon
Those things in itself
Make me thank you
I just don't know if there's more for me
Or this is it
I don't know what to do

~talk to me God

There was a moment
When you held my hand
The whole ride back
We were silent
But the music was playing
The vibe was perfect
Everything just seemed right
I knew I could do this
To be with you
For the rest of my life

I envision this perfect world
Where things just clicked
All my hard work
Finally things started to happen
The woman I let pass
Doubled back
And said God sent me for you
No procedure needs to be done
Then comes a son
And a daughter comes after
But it's not a perfect world
And my dreams
I'm still chasing after

~ a perfect world 2

I was running low
People could see it
I was moving slow
The smile they couldn't see it
I was ready to go
Tired
Then I sat down
Ate some good food
Laughed
Talked some shit too
My smile was back
I kept moving
I needed a recharge
I got it too
Much needed
I felt defeated
And didn't know
Where to turn to

~recharge

First off, I have social media
So this test is unwarranted
Can read all you want
Yet
You rather do this shit
Stay bothering me
Working my nerves
But I guess it's a good thing
Because I get to see you walk away
A capital letter B
But it's turned
So I'll let this slide
I'll give you a sample
Don't ask me again
Unless you're bending over after

The music starts playing
Everything was beautiful
The crowd is applauding
They said I do
They were still kissing
The bridesmaids and groomsmen
Were smiling
Everyone walking out to take pictures
The bride and groom stood in front
They all put something on
Hood pose first
They all have their grills on
It's a start
To the party going on

Understanding timing
Allowing myself to be
Working on my overthinking
Allowing things to be
Not taking things for granted
Enjoying these minutes
Not running from
Running to
What am I running to
Well

Just be
Enjoy
Live
Pray
Love
Just be you
A father
Brother
A son
A mother
Sister
A daughter
A friend
Just be what you're meant to be
A writer
A painter
A musician
A dietitian
A vet
Whatever
This is your life
Don't just let it be whatever

I like to cut up
She likes to join in
Sticking my finger in her mouth
Sucking on it
Before I nut in it
Letting her sit on my face
Before we start anything
Her telling me to pull out
And put this dick in her mouth
Letting her taste her off it

Can we get away
Put the phone down
We can answer it another day
All the stresses life brings
Leave it behind you
Let me take the stress you have
Of you
Let's just get away
I already have it planned out
Just pack a bag
I'm on my way now

The conversations went long
Interesting
I felt like talking
She was interested
No pause
All conversations
Smiling
Laughing
Intriguing
I learned something
I wanted to keep it going
But my eyes started closing
Let us do this again

When Wayne said
I am a headache but they love the pain
I felt that
Only a few get to see that side
And double back
I talk my shit
Can hold a conversation
And make you laugh
We can go on a date after

I thought about my loses
It started with my Uncle Andrew
Yelling at us for jumping on the sofa
Stop
Get back to it
My great grandma died
Remember it like yesterday
Followed by my other
My grandma
And my cousins
I was young
I understood it all too
The worst one was Nate
It changed my life
My big cousin
My ideal
Made me realize I can die
So much lose
I can go on for hours
Thinking about my people
How I miss them dearly

Had a conversation with a friend
About feeling alone
And being lonely
How I'll never be lonely
But I am alone
I think about that day
Text a few
A few came
My best friends
My cousins
My brother
The homies
Stick by my side
Through anything
So I'll never be lonely
Though I am alone

I remember when Boyz N Da Hood came out
The group not the movie
I was too young for that
If it's taking too long to lock up
Bring it back
I knew nothing about that
But in those few minutes
I done it all
Like when duffle bag boys dropped
If I don't do nothing
Imma ball
My McDonald's checks weren't close
But get money

I might be showing my age
Though I'm not really old
Anyway
Listening to Slow Jamz by Kanye
What happened to those days
Always listening to music
That makes you want to fight everyday
Some Marvin Gaye
Some Luther Vandross
A little Anita
I have a playlist for the vibe
Some Leon Bridges
Some Masego
Alex Isley do her thing
I'm just trying to vibe
We can leave the fight
For the workout
Just for tonight

These little women
My sister and two God kids
Stressful but I still love them
Can I be in a relationship
To them
No
My sister just joined in on the fun
She would just say
I don't like any of them
But today
She said she'll be ok
She just have a list of things
I can't say
I can't call her the light of my life
That's her
I can't say she completes me
She did that first
In 98 to be exact
I can't call her the love of my life
Well
Because that's her
I said that's a different type of love
She doesn't care
If the other two were her
They would have made the situation worse
They just don't know
I do what I want
Just have to keep everything to myself

Woman you are too fine
I am just trying
To pick you up while fucking
Look me in my eyes
Slim frame
Nice ass
Breast sitting right
I like that outfit you have on
Let me take it off you
At the end of the night

Baby you are beautiful
I just had to say it
Pitiful is what I am
I left you go
And I hate it
I just can't blame myself
The timing was bad
But I'm trying to double back
Make it better than what we had
And love you the way
I should have

I remember being in elementary
Anything wrong with me
They sent me to you
I remember doing homework
We sat in your room
And you help me with what I couldn't do
My birthday came around
I only wanted one game
And you got it for me too
You're the reason I like Sci-fi movies
The noise machine you had
Calming the active minds
Of boys and one girl
For nap time
Still being there for us
Once we became grown
The reason I take my God parenting so serious
They way you are always here for me
And I'll always be for here for you
I have a secret though
You're the reason I stopped eating red beans
We had that every Tuesday
You thought I went throw it up one day
Took away my snack
And I told myself never again
I know
Petty
Happy Birthday to my nanny

It is crazy how the world works
Did my dirt
Left someone hurt
And the same just happened to me
Yeah
I am sick
Don't know what I am feeling
I am just done
I am ready to go
I am over it all

It is crazy how life works
Can be having a good day
And life plays an uno reverse
Changed the whole trajectory
Smiles turned to frowns
I can no longer feel anything
Just numb

I really do not know how to feel
Nobody making it any better
Scared
Looking all over the place
Trusting no one
Not ever
Fake smiles
Bad intentions
Did I fail to mention
That day started off great
This all this shit happened

Never thought this would happen
To me at least
Walking pressing the button
I do not hear anything
I see one
I do not see the other
Somethings missing
My heart drops
I see glass
My car is miss
And they stole something
Out of theirs

I feel like
This will either
Bring new life
Or
Leave me scared to death
I hope the latter
I'm tired of the losses
I need better
I felt like I did this
I set us up
And I'm the one that loss everything
And I had my loved ones involved
I want to shed a tear
Not here
Not now
But it hurts
I don't know what to do now
Stuck again
I know I was ready for change
But this is not what I wanted
Not this pain

To the point where I can't
I can't just do things just because
Living every moment with a purpose
Can't live in fear
This could happen to anyone
I was just that lucky person
Fear that it would happen at home
They got me out of town
What am I going to do now
Be afraid to move around
This the life God gave me
Yes
I am sad
Yes it does hurt
But tomorrow's a new day
And I still have to live
I still have to go to work
Yes
It does feel like a dream
Hoping I wake up in my bed
And nothing has changed
It's just not how life works
This happened
It happened to us
Not anyone else
Life goes on
I have to continue to live
I was trying to find the good in it
I see none
But what can I do
Deal with it
And keep on moving
It could happen again
People don't move like I do
Our morals are different
But I will pour me up a drink
As soon as I touch that kitchen
I want to break something
I want to scream at the top of my lungs
I can't
What's done is done

I have to move on
I have to do better
Not because of this situation
Nothing I can do about that
Life just keeps on turn
And there's nothing I can do about that
I just have to live better
Because something more could have happened
Shots could have fired
One of our lives could have been missing
But we are here
We are breathing
Kind of shaky
But we are here
We are still kicking
I thank God for that
Will I go back
Probably not
Not out of fear
Just somewhere I don't want to be
That made it clear
Starting at this moment
In this moment of pain
Sorrow
And disbelief
I have to keep living
Doing better for me
I shed a tear
Didn't expect that to happen
Tomorrow's a new day
Let's see what happens

The thought
This would not have happened if
Popped in my head
Doesn't matter if
The situation happened
I just was talking about loss
How that is all I saw
Happened again
Another loss

Give me a redo
Today was one of those days
A bonding moment
We laughed through the pain
Been one of those years
Oh 2023
Pieces on the ground
That was all that was left for me
But still we laughed
The beginning of the day was great
Thought the cobbler was gone
Oops found it by the passenger seat
Can't thank God enough
The situation could have been worse
We still laugh
Though things were taken from us

~taken

Fuck the police
That's how I treat them
Seems like they didn't care
Left us hanging
The report was filed
But that's all they were doing
Yeah
We heard about what happened
But that's not our concern
If your friend doesn't answer
We're moving on from her
Yeah
Fuck us
Scared and stuck
And they're supposed
To protect and serve
Ha
Funniest thing I've heard
Fuck the police
Fuck them
What's the purpose
Don't care about me
Made my situation
Feel worthless

Easily aggravated
Not trying to waste my time
Things can happen
Still sick from what happened
Help me ease my mind
No one could make it
I was not even trying
Someone wanted to pull up
Pass on that
Feelings do not match
I will lay down
And keep crying

Time to work towards the compound
A spot we won't have to leave
Unless we're catching a flight
Here we have everything
No need to run the streets
This moment canceled those things
I want to go to church
I need to pray for these things
Better days
To find my wife
To have this compound
Enjoy my life
This year has been stressful
Who am I to deny that
I need to put work in
Add up these wins
Because these loses
They fight back

The stories never end
The book may close
But the next volume
Comes with a different title
And life goes on
Humbling
The way life hits
And just keeps going
While I'm down on one knee
From a punch to the stomach
Thankfully the cross missed me
And I was down before the uppercut
I got up though
Just hope this next chapter
Brings me something different
In a good way
Tired of this pain
Tired of being hurt
And I feel like it's my fault
On to the next though

3:42
Been in and out of sleep
Feeling sick
Head started hurting
Wishing I had someone next to me
I went buss one
Didn't help me
Though I thought it would
Now I sit on the balcony
This cool air does feel good
But my mind is on repeat
Pressing the button on my keys
Seeing glass everywhere
Nothing
Thank God
There car wasn't stolen
But damn
They hit me
Wondering what's next
Feeling stuck again
But my friends say they got me
I still want to cry
I'm holding everything in
I don't know what's stopping me
My books are gone
Took my gun too
Thank God my bag was at home
I wouldn't know what to do
It was almost on E
Glad I didn't fill it up
Work keys were in there
Not getting that back
Will I get my car
Truly doubt that
I wonder what will happen
I feel so bad
I want someone next to me
Just someone to be here
Shows how lonely I really am
Had to delete the word alone
I'm never that

I pray this levels me up
I'm tired of going backwards
Wanted to go to church in the morning
Don't know how that will work
I'll do some praying here
Hope that works
Just when I felt like I was getting somewhere
Skipped my turn
Tired of playing these games
Remember how they would say
It'll be your own people
That do that to you
They're no people of mine
Mine don't move like that
Stressed
Though I am blessed
I'm still here
I guess
Physically maybe
Mentally
Yeah
That
I've been there before
On a date with the beauty
Thought it was a good spot
Could have fooled me
Broad daylight
Why me
If I was to start smoking
Today would be the day
If I had some edibles
Or some alcohol
They all would have been gone
Today
Right now
I need something
To ease this pain
I feel bad for my friends
Felt like it's my fault
Foolish of me
I love them

Wouldn't want that to happen
To no one
Just was one of does days
Things happen
Wish I had a drink
Something to numb this pain
Send me a sign God
That everything will be ok
I don't see the moon
So I can't talk to it tonight
But damn
This year
I've lost my car
Twice

If I never talk again
If my smile stays hidden
The pain has won
I've given in
The negative been winning
I just want it to be over
So I just go where life takes me
Just riding the Rollercoaster
Not trying to hop off
Just dealing with what life gives me
Quiet
Quiet Place 3
Not allowing anyone to hear me
Done
I let it get to me

It was all a dream
At least I wish it was
It's a story to tell
I wish it was a better one
I still feel sick
Didn't get out of bed
Until after one
COD about to see me
Have to take this pain out
I'm no killer
But on here
I am one

Today I slept all day
Hoping the pain would go away
It subsided a little
But I still feel it
Praying to God
Something good
Comes from this
Still wish I could wake up from this
And it would have all been a dream
But
It is not

Feening for a fix
Something to help ease the pain
At least the notes will be gone
I just was saying
How much I loved my baby
Guess that's what I get
For loving material things
Where's the drinks
I left the edibles
Just me and my feelings
Feels like my heart wants to explode
My stomach sinking lower and lower
I don't know what to do
Follow protocol
Get it over with
And pray to God
Something good comes from this

Last night
I wanted to take a ride
And remember my car was gone
So I sat on the balcony
Hoping to see the moon
Looking to the sky for answers
I know God can see me
I know he can hear me too
He knows that I'm lost
And I don't know what to do
In and out of sleep
Wanting someone next to me
Settled for comfort food
Hoped on the game for a while
The shooting helped my mood
Temporarily
Still wondering why
Still seeing how life keeps going
I maybe in pain
But life keeps going
Thankful for the check ins
My village is the best
Don't hesitate to call
I'll try my best
I'm trying not to go back to sleep
Trying not to lose hope
Praying for something good
Even though
I really don't know
Finally started to feel free
That's all I ever wanted
Then life showed me the truth
The image I never wanted
Don't know what's next
I have to keep going
Really emotional right now
I finally feel the tears flowing
I've been bottled up
Playing hard for no reason
It's been a rough year
This took the cake for no reason

Felt like my world shattered
But my life is still intact
Though my possession is gone
I can replace that
Don't know how long it will take
Don't know what will happen
All I can do is pray
But damn
This really happened
Wish it all was a dream
I know I said it before
Thought I hated the saints before
I hate them even more
Know it has nothing to do with them
The city let me down
The people
The police
Those moments all I had
Were my friends around me
And they had me
Everyone seemed like an enemy
A wolf in sheep's clothing
Though they didn't know
What was going on
Glad we made it home
Though their back window was gone
I could barely hear when I got out
We laughed about it all
Hugs and handshakes
A creation was had upon
This horrible situation
A bond
A friendship
No one could replace it
In this moment I am weak
I felt good for a moment
I thought about it again
Felt sick to my stomach
Another loss
I thought
Why me

I said
Started to look for something else
This shit won't happen
Slowly losing faith
I need a pick me up
I'm trying to do it myself
This weight is too much
My head is starting to hurt as I write
I want to hop back in bed
Missed out on work
Really didn't need to be dealing with that
God please help me
Protect me and strengthen me
Help me find my way back
I pray something better comes
I'm tired of feeling like this
Did I deserve this
I keep saying this my karma
But I really don't think so
I haven't been sowing bad things
I don't see why I would be reaping this though
God you're all I can talk to
No one else could understand
Except for the family that was with me
And they felt that pain
I need them covered
They had a rough year too
I pray for better days
It all begins with you
Though I want to be consistent in church again
The connection starts here
I know I'm praying while writing
I know you're still here
Though it's been rough
I still thank you for another day
Through all the ups and downs
You still have been here for me
For us
Like I said
It could have been worse
We witness the second half

Thank you
Because we're safe
And we couldn't have

I have a story to tell
Wonder if anyone would listen
It wasn't funny at first
But we found the funny in it
Then the pain hit again
Today I found the funny again
They slid
Bust the glass
Took what they wanted
And left the books inside
Not just in one car
But both
I laugh just thinking about it
Sucks that it was our cars though

Can I keep the story going
Flowing like the water in the Mississippi
Wishing death on those who did it
Hatred for the whole city
The smile has disappeared
And if it does appear
It's temporary
I went look at my baby
The pain hit me again
I don't want to look at my baby
Glad they found her
In a better state than I expected
The pain has taken my tongue away
Only talking to those who's close to me
Anger inside
Pressure built up
In search of a release

Life goes on
No matter if the world
Feels like it stopped for me
I may not be smiling
But they're smiling around me
I'm walking around like a zombie
I see them clowning
I feel weak
The clouds are gray
Even though the sun is shining
With no cloud to be seen
Life is going
And going
While I'm standing still

Every time I hear Just in Case
It takes me back to this one day
When a toast was had
Surrounded by
Some of the people I love
I spilled my shot before that
My bad
But my voice was heard
It was a celebration
The shot we took
Dancing we did
How I got home
I don't know
But I did
Just reliving that moment
Every time
That song plays

I look to the sky again tonight
Hoping to see the moon
Many stars shine
But the moon has gone missing
No clouds in the sky
To hide them from me
Questions
Wondering where did it go
Still I look up
Search for an answer
Maybe it's talking to God
About the prayers I need answered

This one star shines brighter than the rest
It's always in my view
Maybe it's a camera
And this is a globe
Like the Truman Show
This time
None of us know
That this is all a game
That's why we can't fly drones
High into the atmosphere
They don't want us to see
Or maybe it's a satellite
Still though
I feel like it's watching me

Through tough times
Just want someone around
Closer than family
Still they hold it down
I could use one of those hugs
From Kyn right now
Always giving me a tight squeeze

191

I cried
Questioning why
I feel like a failure
I feel like my losses
Are building up
And I'll never win at this time
Wondering who am I
When I felt like I found myself
Asking God
What is it
Why I can't get anywhere
Am I supposed to be here
Is this it for me
I needed these tears to fall
I needed this release

I had to talk to God
So I isolated myself from everyone
No music
No light
Just me and a dark room
I can hear the world around me
The buzzing
Of a fly in my ear
Something crawling around me
At this moment
I don't car
The words came out
Tears started to fall
I needed this release
But my questions weren't answered
At all
Hopefully one day
Soon
Because to be honest
I feel like giving up
I know I'm strong
But the weight is catching up
And I'm tired
So tired
My legs and arms
Are about to give up

I smiled
It did not go away
I laughed
A good laugh too
It was necessary
I was down again
Needed a pick me up
I had cried
Nobody knew though
Pick your head up
That's what I was told
They lifted me up
They just do not know

Darin
I love you so much
Through those hard times
You get back up
Even when you're low
You keep fighting
I'm proud of you
I love the fact that you chase your dreams
People might not read
But you're doing it for you
And that's good enough for me
You made those changes
You've started eating right
Still stretching fight
Eat sweets every now and then
But you're still doing right
I love your personality
The way you're always there
I love your smile
You stay smiling from ear to ear
You are you
The reader
The writer
The friend
The brother
The son
The paran
And everything else
You're the best
Your dreams will come
Even though you feel like it won't at times
You will find your love
Even though you feel like you're out of time
Just be patient
It's coming
Just know
I love you
You're doing great
Your time is coming

I dream of better days
When the losses
Finally turn into wins
And all the worries fade
To do all the things I dreamed of
To find love
To push the grand national on Sundays
To take random trips with the crew
Two weeks of planning
And then we go
To see my books move further
I have to grow an audience though
Just to live the way my heart desires
That's all I want
To spend my life with one
Until we create more
That's all I want

It's been a minute since I've felt this way
I thought those feelings changed
Tough times brought them back to me
Trying to keep my head up
Thought I got rid of those mask
I found one tucked away
I am not ok
I just realized
I am alone
And I'm feeling lonely

I am drained
Emotional and physical
No need to call my phone
I will be good
Don't need a superhero to save me
Questioning the dynamics of these relationships
Only a few seems friendly
So it is just me and God
Plus the family I created along the way

I had a dream
That I met this lady
She was different from the rest
Her attention I had
Doing things the others never did
She pulled up on me
When I was with the homies
Something I didn't think she would do
She said I was meant for her
I just laughed
Think she had a good game on her too
One day
We ended up at the same place
Didn't know
Until I asked her what she was doing
She asked where I was at
I replied
Just pulled up outside
Saying I'm coming with you when I walk in
Thought she was playing
Trust issues kicking in
Until I walked in with my friends
Met up with my coworkers
A hand slid into my hands
There she stood with her friends
Though it all was a game
She showed me otherwise
We went sit outside
Talked until our friends
Slowly came outside
That's when the fun really begun
Then I woke up
Upset
Dream me
Found the one

As I sleep
I dream more
Movies it feels like
Taking me away
From the thoughts of real life
So I sleep more
The dreams feel real
Until I wake up to real life
And I'm drained
Just wanting to sleep
Sick of reality
I rather live in my dreams

In life
Change is inevitable
Can spot it in a face
But the best thing in the change
Is the consistency
In those people that change with you
Making life
Easier to go through

I haven't seen any birds in a while
Where did they go
I watched a Ted talk
Said they killed them all
Is that why
The sky isn't filled anymore
Life doesn't seem the same
Since I've grown
Except the games being played
Though I left that at school
A long time ago
Making jokes about everything
Damn
B.G. just came home
I like to laugh to
But to put a label on someone
Because something don't sit right with you
I try to stay off
I have to get these writings out
Though people don't care to read
Did love disappear with the birds
I shouldn't have cheated in my relationship
Been afraid when the opportunity came again
Mistakes
Remember when we use to get two hot n spices
Only ketchup and cheese
Two dollars and some change
I don't even eat fast food now
But those prices are crazy
Went to target the other day
Just for some fruit
Twenty dollars gone already
Prices steady going up
But these wages stay the same
They say nothing is certain
But death and taxes
Seems like that's all we work for anyway
Just to go without actually living
Though some people found a way
Living over existing
They found a way

Change is inevitable
Don't want to get left behind
Have to adjust to the times
The best thing about change
Is the ones that change with you
The ones God sent
Even when we bring in the wrong people
And they go
Their love stays strong
Like mine after my car was stolen
Thought I hated the Saints before
This is more ammo
With a charger
Goes to show how creative people are
But that's how they move
Lost
Almost made me hit the blunt
Stressed
But I said no
Hidden feelings revealed
True intentions come to
Conversation I want to have
But an Instagram post is more important
I rather talk to myself
Most time I talk to God
And at night when I'm outside
I talk to the moon

Time
Too much time
Broke the bond
Space created by your mind
Wanting things to be the same
But you forced my hand
Understanding you did it on purpose
Didn't make thing better in the end
Months go by
No replies
So I let the text die
Then those feelings went away
We remain friends
But what we were creating
Has come to an end
Forcing a change
And time has taken away
Everything

How quick the name changed
The ink already dried
The wounds healed
Just another story to tell
The blackjack exploded in hand
The pain was real
But no scar was left
Just the memory of something
I thought would last forever

In my time of weakness
I was alone
Not discrediting my friends
My family that checked on me
But those women
That want to lay with me
The ones that come and go
As they please
Didn't say anything to me
Now they come back around
Not trying to exchange energies
I'll just stick to me
My alone time was a part of my growth
Had to see what was around me

I want to get away
Leave behind everything
Get a breath of fresh air
No specific place
Just me and the world
Life around me
Will be the only music
That plays

I am dreaming more
Forgetting them as soon as I awake
Starting to seem more and more
Realistic
Wishing I could stay
My subconscious is teasing me
Knowing when I open my eyes
To no surprise
I have none of those things
So I rather dream
Sleep my day away

It is crazy
How two random men
Can bond over a fat ass
I glanced as she passed
Then watched her walk away
Just to look up and see
Another man
Doing the same thing
We laughed
Both said damn
And went on about our day

The most beautiful thing in my life
At this time
Is the sunrise I catch
At 6:39
The orange rises
Turning the black sky
Blue
Leave the clouds that covered
Gray
And me thankful
For another day

You're not the type of vibe
I'm trying to be on
Honest with myself
I'm a catch
You've been sleep on
Games you play
This ain't 2k
This something
You can't see me on
Though you can't see me in that either
See you want to play
Run around and come back in my face
Then see I turn up my face
Go back the other way
Hoping things will be the same
Until you see someone else
Standing in your places
Smiling

One day I want it
The next I do not
I want someone in my space
Next moment
I need you gone
Don't mean to be rude
My social meter is drained
I need my space
People leaving me drained
So I want my own space

I wanted to throw my phone
Out of anger
Hurt
Tired of being alone
Tired of seeing the things on my phone
Living life
Through this phone
I want more
I'm trapped again
Stuck in one place
Just me
Feels like I'm in Abby again
A box
That I've finally escaped
Just to be in another
In another place
Expecting to grow
And I've grown
It's just that
Now
I see more things
I feel more things
Things happening more
Worse than before
My temper flares
Not like before
Breaking everything in my room
No
Not like before
I controlled it
Though I wanted to throw it
Leaving pieces on the floor
Just like
How I was left
In need a release
Separation too
Overwhelmed
Out of control
Working my way back
I just need more
From me

213

For me
This world can't do it
I have to do it
For me

2023
Been testing me
And my team
A bunch of losses
Pain
And tears this season
Hell
This year
I feel like it's for a reason
Raining on our garden
So our harvest
Will be fruitful
Next season
Though it feels like we're drowning
Killing what we planted
But I can see a stem and leaf
Growing through the seeds
Our win is coming

For a minute
I was done
Tired of meeting new people
For what
Take too much
To meet new people
Getting to know new people
Small talk
Questions
Over it
Done with it
But I feel that changing
I am ready again
Maybe just for networking

Sometimes
I look for the words to say
To start off these thoughts I have
So I don't write
I talk to myself
Placing myself in solitude
I can be easily distracted
A message
That leads to a scroll
Then to ESPN
Don't have to worry about a phone call
People don't do that anymore
Barely respond to a text
I guess that just goes with the times
Everyone has their phone in their hands
But I digress
What does friendship mean to you
Do we have to talk everyday
Are we friends if we don't trust one another
I mean we're grown
We're busy
Does that mean we don't love one another
For me
If we're locked in
We're locked in
Only you can change that
We can go years without speaking
Doesn't mean the love won't be there
Back like we never left
But if your placement is temporary
You show your true colors
Then try to come back
Friends turn to associates
Better be happy with that
We're too old for games
Your feelings begin fake too
If I can't trust you
I can't fuck with you
That's all it is to it

Quiet as kept
When it comes to women
I sometimes
Don't go after what I want
My confidence is usually high
I'm a great guy
But social media
Shows that's not what they want
Then I'm not where I want to be
Still grinding for my place
No one I want
Is going to want to grind with me
Established is what they need
I'm too old to be grinding
Find a place and settle
Get what you're supposed to have first
That's the only way
To me that's miserable
So I don't even chase
The DMs stay empty
No text coming in
But from women
That I know
Will never be anything

Who is with me
Though I feel alone
God is with me
Though it's still quiet in my room
Day comes
My phone rings
Two separate things
Relationships I need
And those I don't
The ones that fill me
The ones that make me fill alone
Who is with me
When those stressful days come
Phone rings
Those that check in
Those that don't care
Their true intentions
Shown with every message
God shows their true colors
Though I go back to them
Allowing me to feel alone
Where I need to be
To show me
What's really going on
When my head
Battles with my heart
When my head wants
To keep these people around
And my heart
Wants to love those
Who love me

Every morning
I look in the mirror
And every morning
I like what I see
There was a point in my life
When I hated me
Walked away from the mirror
While I was brushing my teeth
Hated me
So I didn't smile in pictures
Hated me
When I smiled
Delete that picture
Hated me so much
I didn't deserve to be happy
I didn't deserve good things
I hated me
I no longer feel that way
I cringe at those days
Took a while for that love to show up
I'm glad it came
I can't love someone else
Without loving me
And I love me
More than anything

Hard times came
Destroyed the house
But the foundation stayed
Because I built it with God
And everything will be ok

Woke up early
Restless nights been around
Felt like I just went to sleep
But I took advantage of it
Grabbed a book
Hit the balcony
Read and watched
The sun warm the earth again
Until it became a little too warm
I had a hoodie on
And in my room I read
Brought a smile to my face
But that wasn't the best thing
Turned on my TV
YouTube on my firestick
Kirk Franklin popped up
And praising God I did
I cried on the first song
My Life Is In Your Hands
The one thing I've been missing
Something that relates to me
In my room
I continue to praise him
My favorite song came on
Why We Sing
Balling
I Smile
Melodies From Heaven
I have this warm feeling
Through this storm
I can make it
Not because of me
Or anyone else
But God

The sun shined brighter today
I felt this warmth in my heart
Tears ran down my face
No
I am no longer sad
Joy filled my spirit
Giving God his praise
I've mistakes
Questioning everything
But today
I know fasho
I can make it through
Any and everything
With God

Every time I hear
Gonna Be a Lovely Day by Kirk Franklin
It brings me back to vacation Bible school
When I had a crush on this one girl
And Nate told me what to do
When we had to perform the songs
The fear of speaking in front of people
Started in those days
But I had my brother and cousins with me
My aunties there
That's at Calvary
MBC was different
Talking too much
Boy I know your daddy
I met one of my best friends back then
Later found out she is my cousin
Been locked in ever since
Clearly
She's one of my best friends

For a while I was looking
For a song
Or an album
To make it through these workdays
Stressing over their actions
When they will not say anything
Until today
I realized
Gospel
God will help me
Through my days

If I call it blessed
I'm talking about me
For having you
I see the checkered flag
It's the end of the race
First place
None before
None matters after
But this ain't NASCAR
And I probably have the analogy wrong
Just give me my flowers
Champagne too
Use that to celebrate
The vows for us two
No sense of waiting
I love what I'm seeing
I can't play games with it
Miss out on my blessing

I have a taste for success
I see a plate of it coming
It smells delicious
God has set the table for me
I just had to be patient and wait
He didn't make it just for me
Also for everyone I'm with
Before we eat
We hold hands
And bow our heads
Sending up a prayer
Thanking him
For what we're about to eat

The year is 2107
We're under a dictatorship
AI has taken over
And they put Trump's consciousness
Into one of the robots
Taking over more than the United States
We've been fighting back
But it seems like our efforts aren't enough
Each governing power
Has brought back the consciousness
Of their leaders
It's horrible
Their weapons
Have surpassed bullets and missiles
I've witnessed a society
Wiped out in seconds
If it wasn't for the message we sent out
Into the universe
We wouldn't be able to protect ourselves from this
We've moved to a secret location
Off the grid
But I don't know how long will it last
People are bringing in our technology
That will make it easy for them to track us
I get they miss their families
But it's destroying our protection
We've had to move several times
The ones on the outside
Has either chose to serve
Been forced into slavery
Or been killed
We've been fighting to free them
Failure is more successful
Than our actual success
But at least we're trying
Tomorrow is our election
Our great leader died
In the last society evaporation
Trying to save the children
I was there
I don't know how I survived

228

But there's always a few
With that
They believe I should be the next leader
Of the Revolution
I don't believe I'm ready
Someone else is more qualified
But I can't sit here and do nothing
I know more about the fight
They will vote in the morning
I know the other candidates
I hope the best one wins

For the longest
I never thought I would be heard
My words meant nothing
The post would go
Unlike
Not shared
I'm posting them
For nothing
No one cares
Until I went somewhere
And one day
Not just one person
Everywhere I turned
Another person
Told me that love what they see
They need more
It's motivating
I needed that
Didn't think anyone was listening
Thought I was going unheard
My voice was trembling
But they hear me
I was wrong
They hear me

Life is life'n
The losses are adding up
Tears filling up the faces
Pain too hard to overcome
Where are my prayer warriors
Before we drown inside these cups
Can't speak on change
Nothing is ever done
So they take it into their own hands
Then the cycle continues
The tears continue to fall

My space feels like another world
Outside of it feels cold
So I run back into mine
To recharge
Allowing someone to visit
I'm skeptical
Bringing someone in
Destroying my peace
When I should have peace at home
So I stay alone
Stepping into the world
With a peacoat on
Searching for warm souls
Making this world
Tolerable

Idea
Comparing mental frustration
To being sexually frustrated
Hot and bothered
To seeking knowledge
Not wanting to deal with just anyone
But we settle
Not fulfilling that need
Not scratching that itch
So you search for videos
You read books
Still
You have needs
That's not being met
Craving
Angry
Tired of waiting
But these people on other shit
Horrible mindsets
Fucking anything
Don't want my soul attached to that
Comparison
Seem the same to me
Though for me
The conversations
Turn me on sexually
Physical attraction
Can't be the only thing
Not just trying to fuck anything

In the midst of
Closing some of these door
Too many have access to me
Keep going back that way
Never receive my blessing
Feels like I gave them
Them the key to the lock
Just to do the same things
Shame on me

It was the games she played
That stopped a real nigga
From fucking with her
Listening to her friends
Thinking I'm doing something
I wasn't
When I spent every day with her
Jealous ass women
Only because they want the dick too
But I am only fucking you
Was fucking you
She lost out that
Allowing others
To be a part of what we had
No need to fight for this
You had your chance
We discussed this before
But you brought it back
Now I'm moving on
We're too old for that
Or maybe I am
And you haven't grown up yet

Silent
Is how I feel
Silence
Is what I want to give
But I have to put a mask on
Get my laugh on
To make it through these nights
Woke up out of sync
The Rollercoaster took a dive
This morning I was high
Went to sleep and changed everything

For if I die too soon
I want to write letters
To all the people that I love
Expressing myself
But that would take so long
Because there are just one or two
Those one or two
Might have had
One or two
And I love them too
So I get tatted
Or send a message
Never been afraid to give out flowers
Just don't want it to be too late
For them or me
Because anything can happen
To them or me
And they'll never know
What they mean to me

If I could go back
To a certain time of my life
I will walk into my grandma's house
Kiss her on the cheek
Lay down on the sofa
And watch TV
Young and The Restless
Price is Right
Supermarket sweep

If I could go back in time
I will live in that moment
You me and the night sky
Food being delivered
A breeze
Reminding us that fall has come
You wrapped in my arms
Giving you a place to be warm

Just poured a cup
Of crown apple and pineapple juice
Not just any cup
My favorite one
My yeti pie worked on
With her favorite writings on mine on it
Thank you

So much going on
My mind on go
I should have taken an edible too
But I'll save that for another time
Already trying to find release
In the bottle of this cup

Life is such a Rollercoaster
The highs and lows
I've always hated those rides
Only one person got me on those rides
If I knew life would compare to it
I would have never got on

I cried the other day
Sunday to be exact
Worshipping God
Felt like he was what I lacked
But is he fed up with me
Blessings he sent me
I didn't cherish them like he asked
I'm ready now
I don't think he heard that

Life keeps going
Watching the kids
That I watched
Grow up
Like what am I doing
Besides getting older
Played games until I was older
Is it too late now

One cup down
Ice
I may need more
But my yeti is already cold

Does the words
Scary and lame
Still hold weight at this older age
Shouldn't have mattered then
But I've always been out the way
Still I feel like nothing changed
Still a popularity thing
Though you may be cool
You don't do
What I feel is acceptable
I can't fuck with you
Thank God I found my people

Energies match
Dating
Good luck with that
I rather play with myself
Using my left hand
Instead of my right hand
And I'm left handed
But I write enough about that
I'm not settling
That is that

What cup number is this
I lost count
Next

Sometimes I want to ride
Late nights
And be high
At the same time
But I tend to see colors
Can't be alone on these rides
But there's no one
To vibe with

241

Hold conversations with
To laugh with
So I roll alone
Ready to meet new people
But these overnights
Killing my soul

God what is it
Am I doing something wrong
I know I've changed
And the more I change
The stronger the battle
I'm tired of being a strong soldier
I'm ready for the more you have for me

Look
Someone is texting me
Dick is all they want from me
Can't they see we're talking
A lean piece of meat is all they see
I fall in that trap sometimes
I wouldn't even call it a need
If I'm not mentally stimulated
It doesn't even arouse me

I'm going in and out
I won't make it
I want to cry right now
I can't fake it
I fucked up a lot
I know that
The falls I had
I deserved that
But I'm still falling
I deserve better
I'm doing better
What's next

Sleep I guess
I put the cup down
One last sip

Love I want
Dreams I chase
Even into this older age
In God I have faith
Praying to him every day
Family and friends I cherish
Past I leave
Present I live
Future I hope to be better

Goodnight

17
Upset
I can't wait to be 21
Can do what I want
21
Can't wait to be 25
Ready for my insurance to drop
25
Too close to 30
I need time to slow down
30
It's not as bad as they say
Have a different perspective now
33
Thinking about what I'm missing
Cherishing more now
40
Not there yet
Hopefully I've figured it out
Got away from the bullshit
On to different bullshit
Adding it to my garden now

I've had enough
This place has become a bore
I'm tired of doing these same things
I check to see if anyone else is around me
And I take off
No I'm not a superhero
Yes I'm super
But I'm just a black man that's not from here
See we came here to observe the planet
To try to learn them
And help them grow
Didn't work
All they wanted to do was steal from us
Kill us
And everything we created
They wanted to call their own
Throught the centuries
They brainwashed us
Made us forget our power
Place us in one region
Though that's where we landed
When we first got here
And treat us like we were aliens
But once I look up into that night skin
There's always this one star that shines the brightest
I feel like it follows me every night
Though I pay it no mind
Until tonight
I turned the music off and put my phone down
The way they controlled my thoughts
And just listened to the world around me
Looking into the sky
The star found me
It was playing a message
A visual that only I could see
Helping me remember who I am
And what my mission was
I remember now
I always wondered why the sun gave me strength
The moon gave me wisdom
And the rain recharged me

245

Giving me peace
And the star is my home
A planet called RTP2
And I'm on my way home

For a while I was thinking about stopping
Not writing
But sharing them
Publish this last book I'm working on
And burying them
Deeper and deeper into my files
Until tonight
A lady came bragging
Saying how she loved it
And shared it with her kids
Even told me her favorite
Titled What If
As soon as she said it
I remembered
I needed that
And when I publish this one
I hope she sees this

Mind drawing a blank
Body feeling ill
Don't think I am sick
Drained is what it is
Need me a break
A break outside of my box
Hopefully with someone
That will lead to a good time
No I am not talking sex
I'm talking conversations
And laughs
Talking underneath the stars
Though I don't see that happening
I will enjoy my own company
I need a recharge
I need to feel like me

It was just a summer thing
You and me
Thought we never done anything
You and me
I caught feeling
You ran away
Nothing left to say
Now fall is coming
The weather's starting to change
Now there's no more
You and me
Not even as friends
No you and me

I want you around
Trying to lay you down
Penetrating your mind
Body
And
Soul
With my tongue
Alone with these strokes
Let out those moans
I'll say something in your ear
I want you to cum
Your legs shaking when you near
Let's make it last
We have time
Two or three rounds
We'll sleep good tonight

I am not in the business of motivation
Everyone does this
I am bringing understanding
Understanding that you are not alone
Someone is going through the same thing
We'll get through it
And motivation is gained
That adds to it

Let us talk
Something that I stand by
The words
Locked in
If I fuck with you
I fuck with you
Something I stand by

She reached her hands in my boxers
Instantly I got hard
Don't take much for her
Pulled it out
Straight into her mouth
Wet and sloppy
Trying to make me nut for her
She must have missed me
I have a surprise for her

We're sitting on side of the moon
How high I feel with you
We sit
With star all around us
Both looking down
Until
We locked eyes
She reached for my hand
Locking our fingers in
I reach for her face
We kissed
With an explosion
Another planet was created
Beautiful colors fill the space
Rearranging things
Our eyes lock again
See the world in her eyes
My sacred place
Wrapped in my embraced
We look into the moon

Never thought this would happen
I'm crying before it happens
The fellas and I prayed
Before we walked out
A toast to love
Now I stand here
Waiting on
You
The song plays
Everyone stands up
Her you come
Beautiful
I have to take my glasses of
Where did this tissue come from
I can't take my eyes off you
When you and your father
Walk up
I notice that you're crying too
I shake his hand
I take your hand
To face each other
To say our vows
To each other
To God
And our family too
I do

I wish you were here
I drift off
When I was in between your legs
Your legs up
With me pinning your knees
To the bed
Slow stroking you
Looking into your eyes
Only hearing you moan
And how wet it is
As I stroke
I snap out of that trance
See a text coming in
You're thinking the same thing
Now
I'm so anxious

She's mad
It was something I said
I reach for hand
She pulls away
Walks to the kitchen
I walk behind
Sitting on the island
Still trying to talk to you
Nothing
I just look at you
Beautiful
Big t shirt
Hair tied up
Some long socks
I hope off the island
Grab you
From behind you
You talk your shit
Talking about don't touch you
But you face me
I kiss you and say I'm sorry
You say ok
Kiss again
And say
I'm still mad at you
I'll make it up to you

First day of spring
It's beautiful outside
Dropped the top on the old school
Headed to pick you up
Opening your door up
You have this yellow sundress on
Think I have a new favorite color
I hear the music jumping
The park is packed
Back the whip in
Open the door for you
Grabbing the drinks out the back
Look at that ass in that dress
Hug coming in
From my little cousin
Haven't seen him in a minute
Getting greeted by the rest
She walks away
To go dance with my momma and them
That ass again
Getting pulled away by my brother
Time for shots
Surrounded by my cousins
Where my best friends come from
Cheers
Who's on the grill
I need to eat something
My auntie grabs my hands
Saying come dance with her
Let me move my feet
She spots me dancing
And dances near me
Smiling
Did I hear something about food
That's just how we roll

She's dancing in the mirror
Getting ready for a night out
A girls night
I'm watching from the other room
Soaking in the beautiful view
Of you
Grabbing the Polaroid
Calling you name
Just to snap a picture
A smile comes after
I want to take off your clothes
Just to watch you put them back on
But I know how you feel
When you're putting makeup on your face
So I'll take what I can get
Kissing gesture
And a wink
Sexy ass woman

I told you my point of view
Let me tell you hers
She was ready
Finally going to my hometown
Dressed to match
And tonight
It's going down
We're throwing a party
Just a family get together
She only met a few
Now she gets to meet most
And my parents too
I met hers a few months ago
Lately we've been too busy to
So we're turning it into a surprise
We get to the hall
We meet with the crew
She went inside to introduce herself
She wanted to do it alone
In the darkroom
She shines bright
And that's not just my opinion
My cousin said
Everyone turned their heads
As soon as she walked in
Questions about who's she looking for
People trying to get her number
Foolish
Found them
And she approached the table
She introduced herself
Excitement from the table
My sister already knew her
She got hugs from the table
A friend of my sister
She agreed to be
Until she saw me walk in
She said all that went out the window
My man my man
She walked away from the table
Straight into my arms

I said I was coming to the table
She said wherever I'm at
She wants to be there
Telling me how happy they were
To meet her
Finally a daughter n law
I said they could keep her
She goes back and tell them what I said
Snitching already

I love the smell of rain
It's Intoxicating
Even better
When I get caught in it
I don't care if my clothes get wet
I'll close my eyes
And embrace the raindrops
As they fall upon my skin
Cold drops
Cooling the heat from my skin
I'll stay as long as I can
I don't get sick
But if I do
It'll be worth it
Enjoying the rain
Falling from heaven

The idea of dating
In 2023
Is surrounded by the bag
Where is the simplicity
She could have
Everything I have
Including the last name
But those things have changed
Goes with the time I guess
Influenced by others
Maybe the screen
And the music too
But I look
For someone who wants me
For me
And then I'll figure out the ways
To provide for you

I admire her drive
The passion in her eyes
Her child will never see her struggle
Though some nights
She has tears filling her eyes
Wine fills her glass sometimes
Failure is something
She doesn't want
Time for a man
Just to be a distraction
Focused on what lies between her legs
Not her dreams and aspirations
Not trying to date
Those games
She doesn't play
An angel
In a world full of demons
Scheming
Surprised it hasn't tainted her soul already
God on her side
So she's protected
Still going out
She's stepping
Lighting up a room when she stepped in
Leaving an impression when she left it
She's a blessing
Ambitious girl
Handling her business
Never quitting
She's catch
Not everyone could catch

I like getting high
It just has me thinking about life
Like
The shifts in life
How I was once a kid
Looking up to adults
Now I'm an adult
With kids who look up to
Damn
What a switch
Like how I've been through
The 90s
00s
10s
And now we in the 20s
To see the colorful clothes
Turn into baggy
Then skinny jeans
I don't know the style now
For me it's hoodies
And basketball shorts
Occasions are for dressing
Seeing the different sized TVs
I miss my heavy ass TV
Made me feel strong when my momma
Asked me to move it
Or even the computers
I remember the green screen
Floppy disk for games
I had to use a typewriter
For schooling
I wonder where I can find one
Someone get it for me for Christmas
Maybe
Anyway
I think about balance
People in your life
Who balances you
Like a Libra scale
It is September
Damn

Let me get back to what I was saying
Balance
Chill
And
Turnt
That's who I am
I have a mix of that
Then life in general
Like how we play with it
The given to us
We're making a shame of it
Because we're a creation
From God
We're supposed to be creating
But we've become clones
From false Gods
Destruction of creation
I mean damn
We hate each other so much
Want to own everything so much
Money goes
As quick as it comes
And the rich pockets keep filling up
Like what are we giving us
We were gift it with talents
But we hurt each out
Into not using them
A lot gets through the system
Still
Look at what we are missing
I even thought the other day
About death
Like what would heaven be like
I know I read the Bible
And what it tells me
But what if my heaven
Is what my mind creates it to be
Creating a combination of things
That will loop me forever
Maybe this life is a dream
We're reliving our lives

266

In a different way
In a different world
In another galaxy

I'm taken to the 90s
Looks like we're in my house
I like the dim lighting
Shades on all the lights
Looks like the shadows dancing
But it's different
People are dancing
But they have pajamas on
Wine glasses on counters
Games on the table
Laughs happen
Hugs and kisses too

Wrote nothing today
In too much pain
Back been hurting
Went too crazy
Woman wants to see me
Too messy for me
Rather stay in my zone
Comfortable
Resting my back
For my next session
So I can do it again

The camera pans around
They're talking
Laughing
Empty plates knocked off
They're talking shit to each other
Pointing
Drinks pouring over
Their lights are dim
The movie playing
Nobody paying attention
The candles burning
Intoxicated by the aroma
Supposed to be playing a game
The conversations took over
The camera pans out
But the scenes isn't over
The laughing is still going
Laughing over
And over

October's
First Quarter Moon

Yesterday took the cake
Gun almost drawn
On a parking situation
Nigga got out the car looking crazy
Bag in hand
Headed to the driver side
Anger
It was her fault
She was in the wrong
She shouldn't have turned like that
Trying to calm him down
She jumps over
I didn't do anything
If you don't shut up
He's going back to his car now
Felt powerless
Felt the heat
What would have happened
If I didn't get out that seat
She saying I'm trying to get her shot
No
I'm de-escalating things
Who cares who's in the wrong
Our lives were in the balance
Would never put her in harm's way
I'm trying to get you out it

I want to give up
Just stay locked up
Just me
My books
A pen
And my notebook
Give me some fruits
An edible or two
Turning my phone on DND
The music is all it is good for
Just allow me to be alone

At this point
I don't feel worthy
Personality ain't enough
I'm also hard working
But this shit doesn't feel real
Thinking about running away
No longer answering the calls
Or trying to date
Who am I really
Thought I figured myself out
Thought moving was the right thing
Losing more than what I had
Looking for something
Grinding for something
I end up with nothing
I'm trying
But that's all it is

September has been the worse
Car stolen
Life almost taken
Books barely selling
Work makes me feel like
I'm not worth dating
Feeling trapped again
God
I keep praying
I keep putting in the work
Nothing has been changing
For the good at least
It's a new month
Might stay inside
All 31 days
Every time I step outside
Something is happening

I just want to find a balance
A place I can be free
I can move around without wondering
A place I don't have to overthink
I want more
But feel less than
I'm better than this
Yet
Nothing is happening
Never give up
Tatted on my wrist
The pain of getting this
Is less than following those words
I want to give up
Trying for nothing
Hurts
Losing way more
Than I win
But like I said
I'm trying
I want my balance
I want to move freely
They say
My time is coming
Those words now
Just seems funny

I miss my friend
Went from talking everyday
To nothing
But was this person really my friend
Or was I just good company
Someone for the time being
Someone for that season
But I still miss this person
Hope they're doing good
I won't be checking in
I'm not the one that disappeared
But we're still good in my eyes
Nothing bad happened

So close to giving up
Looking for a sign not to
I am tired of looking though
I am tired of trying to fight through
I am overwhelmed
I want to cry
But my pride says
No tears will fall from my eyes

I say a guy walking last night
He was homeless
Just walking through the parking lot
And I envisioned myself
Walking through that same parking lot
My biggest fear came true
I lost it all
Started with my mind
And then came the fall

I've been questioning myself a lot lately
Doesn't feel like I'm worthy
Starting to feel a little crazy
Feels like I have to start settling
Maybe God hates me
Shit is crazy
To still feel alone
Though I have my people around me
Not 24/7
So in my down time
They can't help me
I love me
But at the same time
I'm starting to hate me
And I hate that things
Are heading this way

I just want to break something
Anything
Just looked off the balcony
And pictured throwing my phone
Into that tree
Walk into my room
Pictured putting my fist
Through the TV
I'm angry
I'm hurt
I'm say
I've put on another mask
I'm tired
I need change
Before things
Go the wrong way

She accepted the invitation
She was ready for the ride
She kicked her feet up on the dash
Putting her video down on her side
The music played
She was ready to trade playlist
Told her she'll have to pay
For this concert I gave
Sun up
To sundown
Stops to eat
To put our feet in the sand
Pictures taken
Laughs had
She fell asleep on the way back
The fun was had
Her feet are still on the dash
She grabbed my hoodie out of the back
Street lights flash
Magnifying the beauty
Which is her
Hopefully we can do this again
Or we can start this up
Before I leave this as a dream
A vision
That the music has given me

A random taste for vodka
Like in my 20s
Drinking Taaka
I can feel me about to throw up
Living in Houma
Brought that Mardi Gras one
What was I thinking
We were through
That feeling came with reminiscing
Where did the laughs come from
The judgement
Thoughts about
When my patna came out to me
Asking if we will still be cool
What does what you do
In your private time
Have to do with me
We're still cool
Just know that ain't me
Phone calls from a friend
Meeting up
Because she's crying
Things she's going through
People ended up laughing
I'm here for you
I won't be laughing
Too many people judging
Nobody able to express themselves
Or be themselves
Crown Apple with pineapple
For the adult me
A better version of me
Trying to back away from the laughs
The judgement
Though somethings are funny
And somethings are judged anyway

Thoughts run
But no desire to write
Feeling weird
Sometimes it feels as if
I am running out of time
Just drifting
I let go of the wheel

Oh how fast things can change
I stand by these words
We'll be friends
Until you change things
Because that is usually what happens
Unless something crazy happen
I am not usually the one to end things
But it happens

Can you be more
Than I allowed
These other women to be
Not allowing them
To get that close to me
There's been one or two
Things changed quickly
But I see something different
In you
I know you probably heard that before
And I've played those games before
Those were my younger days
Years passed my hoe phase
My mind and my heart
Are on the same page
We see you as a reflection
Of me
And I would never
Purposely
Hurt me
With you
I feel the same way

Trying to understand my own thoughts
These feelings too
This journey is crazy
Tears
I've shed a few
But I'm still here
I look in the mirror
Love what I see
I lay in bed
Music playing
Thoughts running through my head
Damn
I've grown
Though
I feel as if
There should be more to this
Uninstalled social media
Only on my tablet
I will scroll
Barely get on that
Unless the book is due
Ps5 just sitting there
Collecting dust
Material things
I'm not into
Give me my hoodies
A good book to read
I want to take pictures
Bring back the creative side of me
But this world has been winning
Sorry ass job
Car was stolen
Nigga almost shot at me and a friend
Because of how she turned into the parking lot
I'll just stay inside
I can't deal with these things
I want so much better for me
But the more I grow
Seems like the worst things get
Starting to get the best of me
Sometimes I wonder

What is this
Watching an interview this week
Gave me hope on love
But
I'm tired of getting to know people
I watched one about not giving up
Means I need to get to know new people
These books won't sell themselves
Losing hope again
Been a month
Since I was able to move around
Feeling stuck again
This is Abby
All over again
But when the music is playing
And the dim light
Is bouncing off the walls
I find peace
Understanding who I am
What I like
And one day
Maybe
I'll have someone
To share this with
Maybe
After all
God didn't pick me up
Just to continue to fall
Right

Looking for someone
I can spend QT with
Someone who would
Put the phone day
And have fun with
The blue light
Destroying the eye sights
Brainwashing people
With impure intentions
Though it's good to look at
You'll forget
What reality looks like
Walk outside
Everyone's walking
With their heads down
At the table
The phones are out
Did the conversations died
We're just sending memes now
The apps have taken over
Can we put the phone down
Don't mind when the cameras out
Capturing the moment
But let's live it out
Not getting trapped
By the blue lights
Taking hours out of our days
And wonder how

Your face is stick sketched into my brain
I still feel your lips upon mine
The way we held hands
When I drove you home
The way you didn't want to leave
I remember the phone calls
Lasting hours
Wishing you were lying next to me
I remember when you finally were
The kiss you laid upon me
The way my body felt
Knowing you were the one for me
I remember the way you felt in my arms
You felt like a missing piece
You were what I've been looking for
But it became like a revolving door
And one day
You never returned
I waited to see
If I'll ever see you again
Flowers in hand
But they died
The seasons changed
And I was left waiting
Waiting for something
Someone
I'll never see again

As the world continues to go to war
Overseas
And in our backyard
Families are being destroyed
Prices are being raised
Jobs are ending
People are being underpaid
Hard times are upon
The phone
TV
And games
Are distracting
Processed food is killing
And I'm just waiting
For someone I can spend these days with
Because the end is upon us
Revelations said it
God and love can save it
And with you by my side
We can save it
Well
Whatever we can

Who am I
To think I should be looking
Life has been kicking my ass
And I think
I should bring someone into it
Leave them where they are
Nothing I can do for them
Just someone looking for answers
They can't help with them
Why would they
Not their job
What am I thinking
To get to know someone new
Doing way better than me
Nowhere near
Where I want to be
And I think
I can have someone stand by me
Just keep doing what you do
Being sexual release
Nothing else is coming for you
Just lame

I smile
Hard
Just thinking about the conversation
Your smile
Your personality
It's contagious
Can we talk again
When can I see you
Never met someone like you
Didn't want it to end
But the bed calls
My eyes are getting low
I feel high
And it's all because of you
You made my night
The next day will be made
If I hear from you
I found something I like
A new muse
I'll begin with your smile
My second favorite part of you
Your mind is my first
I want to hear more from you

As the weather continues to change

The phases continue to change

And so does the things I go through

To be continued… Until part 2!

Cover Art:

Artist Trigga

Other books by Darin Jamar:

You Are Not Alone

In Search of Forever

Damaged Goods

Life

Chasing The Wind

Push On

Made in the USA
Columbia, SC
03 June 2024

36161379R00161